MW00585533

DEAR KATHLEEN

DEAR KATHLEEN

On the Occasion of
Kathleen Fraser's 80th Birthday

EDITED BY
SUSAN GEVIRTZ AND
STEPHEN MOTIKA

NIGHTBOAT BOOKS
NEW YORK

© 2017 by Nightboat Books
All rights reserved
Printed in the United States

ISBN: 978-1-937658-68-7

Design and typesetting by Margaret Tedesco
Text set in Futura and DTL Fleischmann

Cover: *For Kathleen* by Hermine Ford, 2015
Frontispiece: Kathleen Fraser in Rome, photo by Jeannette Montgomery Barron

Cataloging-in-publication data is available from the Library of Congress

Distributed by University Press of New England
One Court Street
Lebanon, NH 03766
www.upne.com

Nightboat Books
New York
www.nightboat.org

TABLE OF CONTENTS

In her essay "Faulty Copying," Kathleen Fraser writes: "From as early in my life as I can remember, I resisted others' categories and imperatives, perhaps because there were so many of them. I didn't like being identified too readily or absolutely, nor did I wish to represent anything that could be described of ahead of time." Staying true to that dictum has been at the core of Kathleen's writing, a five-decades practice committed to unveiling new processes and poetic registers. A restless visionary who's long advocated for error and improvisation, Kathleen Fraser stands as a unique and indefinable figure in the landscape of post-war American poetry.

I first learned of her resistance to categories when witnessing her pedagogical approach, which I caught a glimpse of when I invited her to teach a weekend workshop at Poets House in New York City a decade ago. Her instructions to her students were meant to de-stabilize the ground they wrote on; she was not interested in answering their questions regarding clarification, but rather encouraging them to create work from a place of instability, to question their pursuit of tradition and authority. There are no hard and fast rules in the world of Kathleen Fraser.

Born in Oklahoma in 1935, Kathleen grew up in a Calvinist family in Tulsa, in small-town Colorado and finally in Southern California, where she attended Occidental College in Los Angles. Her BA in English Literature from that institution was her last degree. Fitting, I think, to a lifelong student interested in pursuing her own course of study. Moving to New York in the late 1950s, she worked for *Mademoiselle* and took poetry workshops from the likes of Stanley Kunitz and Kenneth Koch. She met members of the New York School, including Frank O'Hara and Barbara Guest, who were especially important to her. She learned, as she said, how to write a *New Yorker* poem and three early poems were published in the magazine. But New York, whether uptown or downtown, was not meant to be her city, and she moved west, first to Iowa City, where she taught at the University of Iowa Writers' Workshop, further still to teach in Portland for a year, before settling in San Francisco in 1972, where she was a professor of Creative Writing at San Francisco State University, founder of the American Poetry Archive and Director of its renowned Poetry Center. She published two books with Harper, but was eager to move away from the polished and witty lines of the New York School to embrace, as she describes, "a listening attitude, an attending to unconscious connections, a backing off of the performing ego to allow the mysteries and mind of language to come forward and resonate more fully." She read deeply the work of H.D., Jack Spicer and George Oppen. Since that point, the mysteries and mind of language, along with the pleasures, have defined Kathleen's poetry.

Starting in the late 1970s, in response to Language Poetry and New Narrative writing, the shape and sounds of Kathleen's poetry changed. In *Each Next*, she considered the role of prose narrative, in *Something (even human voices) in the foreground, a lake*, she tackled the space between what's spoken and what's heard.

She became interested in how the role of error might create tension and frisson, as evidenced in her poem "boundayr," in which a typo makes a new word and becomes the perfect title for a complex poem about color and perception. Starting in the early 1980s, Kathleen began considering the idea of history in her work as a result of her stays in Italy, including the Estruscan sites and Giotto's paintings. She not only engaged the physical world of these locations, but also the language that writers have produced about these works, therefore deconstructing while simultaneously creating a new space of language that processes this history. Most recently, she has gone further into the visual and material quality of language and created her own collages and undertaken ambitious collaborations with artists. Her visual poetics, defined by disruption and indeterminacy, are shaped by her love of and ear for the lyric tradition. In the midst of great excitement and disruption, a rigorous beauty defines her work and her interests.

Kathleen, in addition to her extensive work as poet, teacher and administrator, was also the founding editor of the feminist poetics journal, *HOW(ever)*. The journal, which ran from 1983 to 1991, was edited in collaboration with Beverly Dahlen, Frances Jaffer and, later, Susan Gevirtz, and might now be read as a serial project of critical writing in which contemporary, innovative women poets and thinkers engaged the work of the present in connection to earlier experimental women writers. It created a space for contemporary feminist poetics and poetry that went beyond identity politics.

I was fortunate enough to work with Kathleen on the editing and production of her most recent book, *movable TYYPE*, which gathers four of her artists' book texts along with new poems. In one of the artists' books, *hi dde violeth i dde violet*, Kathleen enlarged, cut up and collaged a straightforward poem written for friend, poet Norma Cole, after a stroke had left her unable to speak. Kathleen found herself "writing from the impossible position of saying something real that might acknowledge [Norma Cole's] situation yet possibly amuse her." As reviewer James Gibbons says of the poem:

> There's no missing the relish Fraser took in assembling this poem-object, with its nonsense, bilingualism, contrapuntal type-sizing and jokey liturgical allusions. And yet its irreverence is never at odds with its aim to be a gift for her suffering fellow poet, and the Easter setting accords with the offering of hope that concludes the poem, cast in a simple and gorgeously lucid utterance:
>
> by unseen hand. Light
> opens over trees' abundant
>
> suspend

During our time working on this book, I relished our correspondence and our meetings, the opportunity to share a meal with her and her husband Arthur Bierman in their San Francisco home or enjoy lunch in New York or Rome. She shows up, a live wire at the center of any gathering, whether trenchant or droll, she lights up a room. She is a dancer in mind and of

3

body, a fearless climber of stairs, a walker of pathways in many cities. Her late-night missives, which often stretch to several pages, contain her powerful images and sonic genius, but also her play with punctuation and typography. Indeed, the letter is central to her poetic practice and letter poems appear in many of her books. Kathleen is passionately excited by the new and the engaged in her own work, but also in the work of her friends. She extends the generosity of her interest in everything things says and writes. As she has written: "From the brink or borderline we call the margin, we are able to create another center... a laboratory in which to look for the unknown elements we suspect are there."

This piece was written for a panel I organized in honor of Kathleen's life and work at the AWP Conference in Seattle in 2014. On her 80th birthday, March 22nd, 2015, Susan Gevirtz and I hosted a tribute to Kathleen that included 15 presenters at the CCA Writers Studio in San Francisco. The event was presented by Small Press Traffic and The Poetry Center at San Francisco State University. This book gathers essays by esteemed friends, colleagues, and students of Kathleen's. It's a testament to her warmth and generosity and a reminder of the vision and influence of her work.

—For Kathleen Fraser

I used to be a dedicated user of 411. Many who read this won't even know what I'm talking about. 411 is the number you *dialed* for information. It used to cost a few cents for repeat use so it was a little indulgence or extravagance. Now you'd just Google instead. As a teenager growing up in LA I'd call 411 to ask the operators things like, "Would you have an affair with the headmaster of your high school?" or "If you were going out to dinner in Santa Monica tonight where would you go?" or "What would you wear if you were going to see Neil Young tonight at the Santa Monica Civic?" I considered this to be information. And I got to know some operators through repeat encounters. I guess I used 411 the way I used the Magic 8-Ball: for oracular consultation with the world outside my bedroom.

So, in the fall of 1983 when my boyfriend came home and told me he'd seen a poster at San Francisco State with the words "Feminist Poetics" on it, advertising a class taking place in the spring, I called 411 to contact the professor whose name on the flier was: Kathleen Fraser.

A little backstory: At the time of this flier sighting I was in my second year of graduate school in the History of Consciousness program at UC Santa Cruz. I wanted to do an independent study on "Feminist Poetics" and my professors, Jim Clifford, Donna Haraway, and Hayden White, had never heard of such a thing and couldn't give me any bibliographic input.

I called Kathleen Fraser. Cold call. She said, "Come over and we'll talk." So welcoming to a total stranger! She served me scotch and "Parmigiano-Reggiano." By the end of the visit I could tell that we would know each other forever. Also she invited me to TA her Feminist Poetics class at San Francisco State. Donna, Jim, and Hayden were all fine with this and it turned out that Donna and Jim were already subscribers to *HOW(ever)* journal, which I had just encountered for the first time via Kathleen.

Fraser was in the midst of turning the syllabus and materials collected and presented by students from the first few Feminist Poetics classes, the first having been taught in the spring of 1982, into a kind of textbook titled *Feminist Poetics: A Consideration of the Female Construction of Language*. A few months after we met she asked me to help her edit it. The syllabus for the class was revelatory for me and many others. It was here that I first encountered the work of Dorothy Richardson (whose work would become the focus of my dissertation), along with many other first encounters. There is so much from the pages of the *Feminist Poetics* book (never published) that I wish I could show you. As one small example, in the third paragraph of the Introduction, which precedes the syllabus, course material and student presentations about the poets on the syllabus, Fraser says:

> These learned prohibitions are largely unconscious, but exert powerful limits upon the writing process — the *kinds* of poems they write or at least consider appropriate to share and claim attention for in class. With few exceptions, women students tend to remain passive (at least in mixed classes) in the first weeks of classroom discussion, in which first esthetic assumptions are asserted and "significant" theoretical questions posed. Until some permission is given to entertain alternative possibilities, confusion over the legitimacy of publically unacknowledged differences — perceptual and structural in nature — acts as a silencing mechanism in many women. Silence insures safety from exposure (looking "bad," being "wrong"), thus denying not only themselves but their classmates the experience of multiple pleasures possible in poetic language and the more complex range of human experiences available. Secrets of the imagination remain secret. And without an exploration of those diverging language needs, the charge that the *poet* should be *witness* cannot be taken seriously.

It is strange when something like the above passage, once your immediate, fresh and urgent present, becomes the past, as this passage and the whole *Feminist Poetics* book, along with my first encounter with Kathleen, have now become. I tell this story and quote the book below as microcosms of a whole Fraser-esque approach that endures into the present. I hope these begin to demonstrate something fundamental about her generosity and openness to the unexpected. For Fraser these modes are dedicated ethical approaches to life, poetics and other poets, especially women. Many many writers of all ages have been the recipients of this m.o. as well as of her ceaseless hard work on so many woman-writer-centered projects, from decades of teaching and mentoring, to decades of editing and guiding *HOW(ever)* into the online *How2*.

In thinking about this Festschrift for Kathleen, I made a stack of all of her books. An envelope fell out of the stack. It is one of those envelopes that they put stamps in at the post office, now yellowed. This was a gift she made me for a long-ago birthday or Christmas. Inside are strips of different lengths of paper with words on them. For example, a few randomly chosen strips I just picked say:

Firestorms, Swan 3 (from Leda's journal)

night's moisture,

everything in its path.

saying goodbye.

still wrapped in

myself with pleasure in

exact strokes,

This envelope gift, container of the deliberate random, is another micro-example of Fraser's making practice: the honor of accident or what she calls "the crime of error"; the work as gift, a way to engage so many others (see dedications on many poems); and the ongoing interest in a crafting of "sense" and song from the debris that filters into our lives.

> still wrapped in
>
> everything in its path.
>
> exact strokes,
>
> night's moisture
>
> saying goodbye
>
> Firestorms, Swan 3 (from Leda's journal)
>
> myself with pleasure in

And on this side of all these years I wonder, what is this story I tell about Kathleen anyway: a salvage narrative repeat of a heroic tale with a female as the star? A maternal hand-me-down where the only public graceful expression is that well-behaved and practiced "female" gesture called "gratitude"? (Men may routinely kill the father to become the authority but most feminists know it's bad strategy to kill the mother — at least in public.) This story is a registration and tracing of a lineage whose daily living *has* had its heroic aspects especially in its insistence on the naming of that which had no name, "feminist poetics," as well as so much else. It's the tale of a kind of beanbag relay in which the long-ago boyfriend sighted the flier, then 411 threw me Kathleen, Kathleen threw me Dorothy Richardson, Kathleen next threw me Barbara Guest because Guest had contact with and great interest in Richardson, then Guest threw me Virginia Smyers, librarian of the Beinecke special collections where the bulk of Richardson's papers are housed (Smyers was previously H.D.'s daughter Perdita's private librarian for Perdita's private H.D. library) ...And on and on. I'm not sure what I threw to whom but hopefully something of use to someone, or at least back to those who bestowed so much in my direction.

In great gratitude I want to offer more than gratitude. I would like to make an intervention between the maternal and the heroic by calling up the maternal as the fierce as well as the generous — to imagine that it is our disagreement, our willingness to argue, that is also a kind of generosity, a kind of tending. I am no longer speaking only personally here but extrapolating from Kathleen Fraser's work to what I think she might wish for women poets. I want also to invoke relentless labor and human frailty in this ancestral-lineage-relay story, because all of this must be included to properly honor Kathleen, her poetics and life work.

How can there possibly be a way to register the luck, or thank enough?

Inverness, October 17th, 2014
With many thanks to Frances Richard

when you concentrate,

It is without mercy,

and necessitates victims,

the flutter through my body,

from the windows of

it burns and eats,

— more lines from Kathleen's envelope gift

A CALL FOR FURTHER STUDY OF KATHLEEN FRASER

SUSAN GEVIRTZ

It started with Frances Richard asking me to direct her toward the best critical writing about KF's work. I could think of very little and so, "for fun," spontaneously, Frances and I began to invent a bibliography listing some of the scholarly inquiries we thought *should* exist. Then we wondered why they didn't exist — and began to think of our invented bibliography as a call, a hopeful inciting of studies that we wished would be or had already been written.

More conversations followed. We talked about the Eighties, canon-making, poets in and out of the academy, intersections of feminist scholarship and innovative poetics, the outlines of poetry circles and the passing-down of social formations in those circles. Our talk was, and continues to be, lit up, adrenalized. Talking in this way about friendship and history begins to fill out the picture we ourselves are in, to remind us how these issues of lineage and intertextuality first came to our awareness. Talking calls up and reanimates the initial epiphanic moments of discovery and their ongoing impact in our daily practices — the "why do we do it" and the "you're not alone" of it. We were realizing, in effect, after KF's example, that private chat over tea and full-dress scholarly achievement exist on a continuum and elicit one another.

KF and her work have become touchstones for us as we think about the time and conditions during and under which she did that work, and about the public naming of conditions larger than oneself — a naming that KF has enacted through her own poetics, as well as through *HOW(ever)*, her discursive writing, her translations, and as a contributor to a critically important archive, not to mention through her relations to a larger community of writers and artists across the years. Being of different generations, Frances and I have also been excited by the parallel and divergent ways we have come to and arranged the stories of our entrance into these arenas of making and naming. We both still register surprise when we feel "I'm related to this" — to one another through this, and to others. We don't, of course, assume this relation once and then rest on it; it cannot be taken for granted. It is necessary to recall it, to call it up and unsettle it, to repeatedly talk about and through it, in order to realize its vitality and necessity and perpetual potential to be re-eclipsed by silence.

As editor and teacher, KF has done the work of lineage-making and institution-building for many years. We take up the tools she has given us with her, for her, about her and beyond her. We are thinking of this Festschrift more as a chapter-break than a culmination — as a retrospective but also prospective (incomplete) summary — a look at work remaining to be done, talk not yet heard.

§§§

Our invented bibliography led me to wonder what KF herself most wanted written or said about her work. So I had her to lunch and asked.

It is a real and true coincidence that while KF and I were talking in San Francisco, Frances was across the bay writing about the visual in KF's work. This choice is not in itself surprising, given that Frances has spent years writing about and attending to the visual. Much remains to be said, furthermore, to do full justice to KF's collaborations with visual artists — which, in turn, is only one aspect of the function of visuality in her writing. Still, when Frances reported on her topic, the happy accident revealed itself to be a call-and-response already in progress.

This "Call for Work" is, then, an extended call-and-response, a continuation of my talks with Frances, a surveying of the territory, a collection of lists towards the incomplete.

§§§

What follows — in the spirit of my "411" is a condensed recounting of what KF said at lunch. Frances Richard's piece on the visual in KF's work follows that, leading finally to, but not included in this collection, our invented "Comprehensive/Comprehending Bibliography on Kathleen Fraser."

LUNCH

Saturday afternoon at the round table at my house.

I ask Kathleen: If you could have anyone write a book about your work, what would it be on?

KF replies: It would be about the visual in my work.

In the Sixties, the New York School poets went to artists' openings all the time. Jack Marshall [KF's then-husband] took me around. It became the excitement — unexpected visual treats of the week... Yes, Thursday evenings. I met Frank O'Hara and we took a liking to each other and he took me to shows in the museum [the Museum of Modern Art, where O'Hara was a curator] before the shows opened. My interest in the visual world got flamed up when I was in New York.

In my work, the visual appeared early on with *In Defiance of the Rains*, which includes prints by Judy Starbuck. Even before that, in fact, *Change of Address* is full of stuff from old bookstores that George Hitchcock found while riding around the English countryside on his motorcycle.

Then later, Sam Francis approached me to do a collaboration. First one of his paintings became the cover of *Notes Preceding Trust*. Then we collaborated on the artists' book *Boundayr*.

Next, painter Mary Anne Hayden wanted to do a collaboration from a selection of the long poem "Etruscan Pages," from my book *when new time folds up*. This became the collaboration *From A Text*.

Then I did *WING* with [KF's son] David Marshall's drawing on the cover and in collaboration with that drawing.

Then *hi dde violeth i dde violet*.

Then painter Hermione Ford and I did *II SS* at the invitation of Steve Clay of Granary Books.

Then after Sept 11th I collaborated with painter Nancy Tokar Miller on *Witness*, at the invitation of Charles Alexander of CHAX Press.

Then *Second Language* with collagist Joanne Ugolini and the printer Don Cushman.

Susan: And in the chapter "Line. On the Line. Lining up. Lined with. Between the lines. Bottom line.," in *Translating the Unspeakable*, you write about the visual in the work of other poets in a way that I think implicates your own work — do you want that implication?

KF: Yes.

• Multiple pathways suggest themselves for considering Kathleen Fraser's poetry and the page as visual space.

• Fraser is a painterly writer, which means among other things that she is *a)* influenced by painters, *b)* interested in color as a definer of form and mood, *c)* involved in the plastic and dimensional relations generated by manipulating a protean material across a flat surface. Print on paper is not contiguous or unified in the same way as paint on a support. But all the words on a printed page are made of print, just as every shape in a painting is made of paint.

• Unless, of course, the painting includes collage or assemblage. Painters who most interest Fraser — from Giotto to Agnes Martin — tend not to introduce such extra matter into their work (though Giotto does use gold leaf). For Fraser, interest in these artists lies instead in a sense of the visual mark as emerging from the body and traversing a distance to hang or adhere on or in or barely above the picture plane: Martin's grids "pencilled over space," or Giotto's O inscribed:

"Not by *system*, but by
wrist,"

"Giotto: ARENA," *il cuore: the heart*, p. 12

• Each of these passages, one in an essay (Translating the Unspeakable[1]) and the other in a poem ("Giotto: ARENA"[2]), folds a reference to drawing into a rumination on painting, and indeed Fraser is as interested in drawing, engraving, and the cinematic framing and sequencing of scenes as in the painterly modeling of form. In the register of the verbal, collage and cut-ups do in fact absorb her attention, coexisting with emphasis on bodily trace as if the genres and mechanisms of representation — from lyric stanzas to personal correspondence, from photograph to brushstroke — were arrayed just a few degrees apart along a continuum. The semiotic/architectonic potencies of paralinguistic marks like lines or dots fascinate this writer, and she exhaustively explores the ways in which varying sizes and styles of type change the cadence or adjust the volume or spatialize the thought-arc of a poem.

• It isn't the same to make a film and to make a drawing, or to paint with oils as opposed to engraving on

> plates [rectangles] of fine-beaten gold…(the size of letter pages with nail holes distributed around their edges, as if pounded into a wooden door or wall)

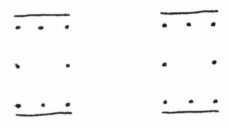

"Etruscan Pages"; *il cuore* p. 111 Fraser's brackets and parentheses

As a visual move affecting the density and rhythm of a page, intercutting a prose passage or a letter to a friend into a spare, meditative lyric is distinct from cutting up a preexisting poem with scissors and arranging its parts on thirty-one large pieces of paper to make a new verbal/visual sequence — a sequence later recalibrated for a regular-sized book:

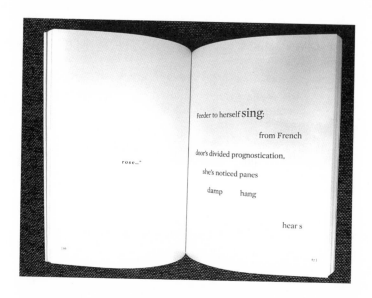

Feeder to herself sing:

from French

door's divided prognostication,

she's noticed panes

damp   hang

hear s

rose..."

Spread from *movable TYYPE.*, pp. 66-67 (*hi dde violeth i dde violet*[3])

• Thus a comprehensive study of Fraser's visuality would catalogue these differences and examine their transfer into poetic text. How does the cinematic apparatus as staged in a poem like "Bresson Project: 'Forget you are making a film'" (for instance) relate to and pull against the drawings that intersperse the stanzas — stanzas that are themselves rectangular, like film frames, yet laid out in a two-page spread in such a way that the poem looks more like a grid than a strip of film, and an irregular grid at that?

Or how do the Etruscan letters in "Etruscan Pages" —

il cuore: the heart, p. 107

—mirror and counterpose the abecedarian lyric lines that precede them?

alpha. aslant. alien. appall. answer. anodic. alum. *A*.

stooping. struggle. squeeze of light. sling. slate. shut.
scrutiny. *S*.

ropy. *R*. viscous. *V*. overhang. *O*. hold. hover. *H*. boar. *B*.
follow. flush. *F*. herbaceous. *H*.

Furthermore, how do periods, and lowercasing vs. uppercasing, and italic
vs. Roman type, add to the interweaving doublenesses structuring this
passage — including the doubling between Fraser writing her poem in
the early 1990s and the Etruscans writing on coins, cameos, mirrors,
monuments, even linen shrouds, a few hundred years before Christ?

• Or take the references to Martin and Giotto. The interruption of
serifed type with handwritten words in the passage from "Giotto:
ARENA" insists on the artist's body (Giotto's, Fraser's or some
intersection thereof) as residual in inscription, irrupting between its
parts — or maybe better metaphors would be percolating through its
faults and porosities, or bleeding through its overlays.

Still, the "handwritten" words are obviously mechanically printed, and
even if the message states "*not* by system, *but* by wrist" — implying
that "system" is cerebral, controlled, mathematical, while "wrist" is
instinctive, corporeal — "system" and "wrist" are made to rhyme in
this special visual way, just as they rhyme in their internal music. Logic
and body are not reducible to one another, nor are they opposed. They
interfuse, and the artist seeks virtuosity in both.

• The O of Giotto is remarkable precisely because its exactitude arrives
freehand — and this is partly what excites Fraser regarding Martin's
grids. Martin, too, drew her geometries without a template, and up

close her graphite line can be seen to quiver as it rides the tooth of the underpainting or registers her breath. For all their clarity and hush, such geometric figures tingle with a vestige of the thinking organism in action, a heat-signature on the abstract artifact. Fraser implies that presentation of the poem and its graphic/geometric elements in print can extend rather than extinguish this scent or tremor emanating from the desire-to-mark. As she puts it in "Translating the Unspeakable," the page is "a graphically energetic site in which to manifest one's *physical* alignment with the arrival of language in the mind" (her italics).

• One glimpses, in such comments, a feeling for the page or painting as a membrane, magnetized to draw gestures toward itself out of the air, gathering the artist's impulse from the space in front of the surface-to-be-inscribed as a photosensitive emulsion gathers and fixes light. At the same time Fraser nearly always implies that the page (or film, drawing, painting, etc.) has an interior, a space inside or behind itself from which the real — urgent, effective — impulses propagate, rippling out to register on the skin of the made object. And, somehow, the page is also thick, as if coated like an etching plate with waxy ground, a tender substance to be scored into:

> as if memory were an expensive thick creamy paper and every
> corner turned now in partial erasure ("WING")

• From this juncture, in the wished-for full-scale essay on Fraser's poetics of visuality, one could talk about Freud's idea of memory as a "mystic writing pad" (1925), a yielding surface accepting intrusions but covered by a protective sheet, which lifts to erase the temporary adhesions — legible marks — whose corresponding scars — physical marks — remain underneath. Then one could cite Derrida's essay "Freud and the Scene of Writing" (1967), which argues that "Writing supplements perception before perception even appears to itself."[4]

Or: another tactic. Discussions of art-surface as dimensional and art-gesture as performative vividly suggest the discourse of action painting —a discourse that, of course, helped to define the New York School aesthetic with which Fraser as a young writer was identified. Harold Rosenberg's essay "The American Action Painters" famously proposes:

> At a certain moment the canvas began to appear to one
> American painter after another as an arena in which
> to act—rather than as a space in which to reproduce,
> re-design, analyze or "express" an object, actual or
> imagined. What was to go on the canvas was not a
> picture but an event.[5]

• Having established some version of these grand bona fides — mapping Fraser's energetic page vis-à-vis psychoanalytic and/or art-historical modernism as well as via deconstructivist theories of textuality — the critic could shift to situating Fraser's visual poetics in regard to late/mid-century literary precursors. Here, by Fraser's own account, a key reference is Charles Olson's topos of composition by field. "Translating the Unspeakable" carries an epigraph from Olson's "Letter to Elaine Feinstein":

> …all from tope/type/trope, that built in is the
> connection, in each of us, to Cosmos…
>
> Place (topos), plus one's own bent plus what one *can* know,
> makes it possible to name.

The "Letter," a coda to the era-defining essay "Projective Verse" (1950), was written in 1959, the same year as "The American Action Painters." Fraser was twenty-four years old.

• "Translating the Unspeakable" explains how the author of *Maximus* establishes and claims the page-arena:

> His cosmos was fleshed-out with double-column
> texts, lists, numbers, historic bits of data, proper
> names, uppercase WORDS, arrows >>>>, slashes ///,
> asterisks *******, underscores, and other enlarged
> graphic symbols as well as lines of type (the typewriter
> being his linotype & personal computer), tilted at
> odd angles or flying across the page, constituting a
> tremendous mimetic attempt to account for the *dynamic*
> physical world as a primary text [her italics].

Cosmos fleshed out through typewriter; physicality as primary text: Here, again, the rational vision that masters idealized geometry and the matter-to-matter impress of signs onto paper fuse; the printed page is understood as both an epistemological proposition and a nervous tissue.

• To name, to write a cosmos into legibility, is not *not* at issue in "Translating the Unspeakable," just as the magisterial fiat of creation is not *not* a concern in "Giotto: ARENA," "Etruscan Pages" or *hi dde violeth i dde violet*. For Fraser, however, creation is translation and translation is kinaesthetic, intermittent, hidden, even violent — subject to disruptions that filter normal sense through time-lag, intimacy, pictures, colors, synapses, silence. (*hi dde violeth i dde violet* was composed for Fraser's dear friend Norma Cole in the aftermath of a stroke that left her temporarily unable to speak. "Writing from the impossible position of saying something real that might acknowledge her situation yet possibly amuse her, I came to an impasse," Fraser recalls. Her answer required the scissors, the thirty-one sheets of paper, and the introduction of expansive negative space.)

• This quality of groping through impasse and lack toward the mark — and concomitant grappling with "the unspeakable" — is what sets the writers named in Fraser's essay apart from Olson. The pages that interest Fraser receive their open-ended, sometimes extra-verbal signs not because the poem is a cosmos willed into being by a sovereign "I" (the first word of *Maximus* is "I" and the last is "myself"), but because such pages serve

> a longing to make visible one's own particular way
> of experiencing how the mind moves and how the
> senses take note. Longing craves articulation and, in
> cases such as these, has sought out visual apparatus as
> scaffolding on which to construct formerly inarticulate
> states of being.

• The cases such as these that Fraser intends are poems by women; the poet who longs to make visible what Fraser calls "the mind's agility, its sensuous diffraction" is female. The full title of her essay is " Translating the Unspeakable: Visual poetics, as projected through Olson's 'field' into current female writing practice." It was written in 1996 and presented as a paper at "Assembling Alternatives," which Fraser describes as a major international conference of English-language poets and scholars particularly compelled by innovative practice. "I decided," she continues, "to trace the path of visual influence inherited by women innovators who connected powerfully to Charles Olsons freeing of the page as a graphic site for poetic composition."

Each essay collected in Fraser's volume *Translating the Unspeakable: Poetry and the Innovative Necessity* (2000), is accompanied by a similar FRAME, a note siting the piece socially and historically. As an archivist, editor and teacher, Fraser is uninterested in fantasies of autochthonic originality. She is, rather, tenaciously attentive to overlaps, borrowings, inheritances, dispersals — further forms of (mis)translation or what she has termed "faulty copying."

• Poets discussed in "Translating the Unspeakable" include (in this order) Barbara Guest, Susan Howe, Dale Going, Laura Moriarty, Myung Mi Kim, Hannah Weiner, Meredith Stricker, Norma Cole, Catherine Bowers, Mary Margaret Sloan, and Susan Gevirtz. The painters Helen Frankenthaler, Nell Blaine, Elaine DeKooning, Grace Hartigan, Jane Freilicher and Joan Mitchell — along with Martin — are mentioned as well, identified in passing as "a second visual source at work" in the development of the feminist-experimental page. One wants to hear more about this composite source and its legacy of workings. (As a start, see Maggie Nelson, *Women, the New York School, and Other True Abstractions*, University of Iowa Press, 2011.)

In these poets' practices, Fraser proposes, "'the mind' of the page" holds contradictory perceptions in tension (Guest). Print-space encodes muteness and "rebuke" (Howe). The poem may, in Fraser's words, "inhabit the present, while marking absence" (Moriarty), and/or explore the ways in which "to claim one's voice would feel *unsafe*" (Kim; Fraser's italics). For the woman poet working with field composition circa 1996, "a distressed and chaotic state" (Weiner) may be notated; "erasing [may become] a way of reading" (Stricker).[6] The field-compositional page transliterates "something perceived, absent, yet elusively there" (Cole), such that "what is uttered into the undetermined and shifting axis hears itself" (Sloan). "As if words changed the second they were committed to paper…as if everything were provisional" (Gevirtz; Fraser's ellipsis), these diagrams of absence activate the written field as erogenous and abyssal, subversive, inessential, interrogative.

"One's own particular way of experiencing" does not, here, guarantee ego consolidation; "one's own" experience is not, as it were, singular or protected by the laws of ownership.

• Fraser observes that the poets she writes about are inventing an idiom in which to track "the very lives that Olson tended to discredit by his act of non-address." With the exception of Kim, these innovative exemplars are white, although Mei Mei Berssenbrugge, Theresa Hak Kyung Cha, Diane Glancy, Harryette Mullen, Sheila K. Smith, and Trinh T. Minh-ha — all of whom were published in the magazine that Fraser founded, *HOW(ever)* — also experiment on various levels with the bodily/graphic/lexical transpositions contemplated in "Translating the Unspeakable."

• "Translating the Unspeakable" analyzes lineage and difference as realized under the sign of or sieved through the mesh of gender. It would be interesting to apply Fraser's historicizing/contextualizing observations to the field-poetic page as investigated by trans writers. (As a start, see *Troubling the Line: Trans and Genderqueer Poetry and Poetics*, ed. T.C. Tolbert and Trace Peterson, Nightboat Books, 2013.)

• Translation derives similarity by testing alternatives; it mines lacunae between synonyms. Fraser's essay accordingly accrues a series of phrases to describe the feminist page(s) she has in mind — her terms rustle together to name the kind of document or texture or location such pages are:

> a 'screen of distance' (apropos Guest's poem "The Screen of Distance")
> a grave of memory
> a forehead
> a lost grammar
> a record of temporality
> a fluid surface of juxtapositions and collisions
> a topos of silence and emptiness
> a slate on which to collage and draw and reconfigure

Each of these phrases in its way fits Fraser's own art.

• Thus perhaps yet another version of the full essay on Kathleen Fraser and the field-poetic page would work backward from the descriptions deployed in her own essay to consider how, across her oeuvre,

> Music was   misplaced
>
> every day,   stubbornly
> its black type,   your hand and
> left wrist   fugal, your deficit
>
> compositional, stepping away
> or away from   pursuit of   place

word worn parties

I spoon was seeking your
separation of mouth's longitudinal
gaze. Music was misplaced

every day, stubbornly
its black type, your hand and
left wrist fugal, your deficit

compositional, stepping away
or away from pursuit of place.
"Placing it where

you see it" plural, veering
into a fixed gaze, I took more.

movable TYYPE, p. 117 ("Second Language")

• In assembling these notes, I find myself recalling Mira Schor's essay "Patrilineage" (1991), which cautions that "works by women whose paternity can be established and whose work can safely be assimilated into art discourse are privileged, and every effort is made to assure this patrilineage." Fraser assures it for her colleagues in "Translating the Unspeakable," and I have attempted to assure it for her via Olson, Freud, Derrida, Rosenberg, even Giotto (and this after cutting references to Dante, Ruskin, Pollock, and Duncan as overdoing it). Perhaps more important, even so, is how Schor's essay opens:

> Artists working today, particularly those who have come of age since 1970, belong to the first generation that can claim artistic matrilineage, in addition to the patrilineage that must be understood as a given in patriarchal culture.[7]

Writing a few years after Schor — nearly twenty years ago — Fraser ends "Translating the Unspeakable" in the same vein: "These bodies of work further extend the visual path to new generations of women poets who will find it more natural to em/body space and its tesserae of human utterance."

I am one of the now very many who can claim this matrilineage, who have been offered a field of em-dashes, both/and slashes, tesseral bodies. For which I send love and honor to Kathleen.

Oakland, October 2014

26

1. Kathleen Fraser, "Translating the Unspeakable: Visual poetics, as projected through Olson's 'field' into current female writing practice," *Translating the Unspeakable: Poetry and the Innovative Necessity — Essays by Kathleen Fraser* (University of Alabama Press, 2000), p. 178. "Faulty Copying" also appears in this volume.

2. Kathleen Fraser, *il cuore: the heart — Selected Poems 1970-1995* (Wesleyan University Press, 1997), p. 122. "Etruscan Pages," "Bresson Project: 'Forget you are making a film,'" and "WING" also appear in this volume.

3. Kathleen Fraser, *movable TYYPE* (Nightboat Books, 2011), pp. 66-67. "Second Language" also appears in this volume.

4. Jacques Derrida, "Freud and the Scene of Writing," *Writing and Difference*, trans. Alan Bass (Routledge, 1978), p. 224. First published as *L'écriture et la différence*, Éditions du Seuil, 1967.

5. Harold Rosenberg, "The American Action Painters," *The Tradition of the New* (Da Capo Press, 1992), p. 25.

6. Fraser cites Stricker's "The Queen Bee" (1988), a collaboration with painter Karen Ganz.

7. Mira Schor, "Patrilineage," in Amelia Jones, ed., *The Feminism and Visual Culture Reader* (Routledge, 2010), pp. 282, 283. First published in Art Journal 50, no. 2 (Summer, 1991).

How to live and work as a writer are questions answerable only by example, and not all examples are equally forthcoming. Of her own example Kathleen has made a public resource, as a writer and a striver after new ways of being a writer, weaving her own aegis out of previously ungathered strands of literary history and exiting masculinist patronage networks to locate herself in a modernist "tradition of marginality." All this she has done without mythologizing that tradition (heroic though it is), working instead to historicize it and her own place in it. This I mean as the highest praise. Mythologies have their inspirational value, but only what is available as history is applicable in practice.

In emulation of Kathleen's candor, I would like to narrate the process that led me to the verses offered here, and my efforts to locate them in literary history. It all began with a book about weather by the Arabic grammarian Abu Zayd al-Ansari (d. ca. 830 CE) called the *Book of Rain*. In the archaic poetry that was Abu Zayd's primary resource, description of the rain is a dominant motif, and in preparing my translation of the *Book of Rain* I began to wonder: Was it only male poets who had anything to say about it? The question led me to Marlé Hammond's 2010 monograph *Beyond Elegy: Classical Arabic Women's Poetry in Context*, which discusses an extraordinary poem attributed to "a woman of the Banu Asad" by the grammarian and *litterateur* Hibat Allah ibn al-Shajari al-Baghdadi (d. 1148). The poem describes a rainstorm coming after a lengthy drought, and with that my question was answered: Arab women poets of old did too describe the weather, or at least one did.

When asked to contribute something in Kathleen's honor, I thought right away of this poem. The translation of an interesting woman's poem from long ago seemed just the thing. But then, with Kathleen's *Translating the Unspeakable* by my side, I began to feel unease. Unmuffling the biographical particulars of women's literary history is such a vital part of her critical work that the idea of contributing an anonymous poem started seeming not so great. Woman's authorship is nothing to take for granted in any period — and if the study of ancient literature teaches you anything, it's not to assume that a female language artist was responsible for the representation of a feminine voice. As a source, Ibn al-Shajari (who says only that "a woman from the Banu Asad" composed the poem) was terribly late. Even Marlé Hammond entertained some doubt about the attribution. Had I, in my enthusiasm, fallen for the *jeu d'esprit* of a latter-day *poseur*?

And so Kathleen's example sent me back to the anthology tradition, where more versions began to appear. "I find great beauty in something said by one of the women of the Banu Asad," remarked one 11th-century authority. On went the search, until in a 10th-century source I was met with the woman of the Banu Asad's name! This was in a poetry anthology by the Khalidi brothers, Abu Bakr Muhammad (d. 990) and Abu 'Uthman Sa'id (d. 999), called *The Book of Similarities and Resemblances among the Poetic Works of Early Islam, the Pre-Islamic Period, and the Generation Spanning the Two*, where it says "Wasna bint 'Amir al-Asadiyya," and then: "These verses are among the most natural of all her tribe's poetic works, and some of the most peculiar in terms of theme. We know of no description of drought and relief from drought that compares to it."

It is a name no other scholar, modern or pre-modern, seems to record. With puzzlement I note that, despite its repeated attribution to a woman of the Banu Asad, the poem is not adduced in Ahmad Musa al-Jasim's 1995 survey of the tribe's poetry, nor included in the 1999 *Collected Poetry of the Banu Asad* edited by Muhammad 'Ali Daqqa. (This modern anthology includes the work of six women poets, alongside the poems of ninety-two men of Asad.) Were the anomalous features of the poem felt to place it outside the pale of classical verse? Or perhaps it was just an oversight. In any case, readers are invited to skip to the end, where Wasna's poem has the last word. What follows here is a partial account of what makes this an extraordinary poem.

To begin with, it presents as a choral poem (a rarity in classical Arabic verse). All first-person pronouns in the poem are plural. A choral performance is furthermore narrated in verses six and seven, which report what a group of women sang on an earlier occasion — the occasion of an istisqā' or "prayer for rain" ceremony whose fictive nature cannot be overstressed. The poem represents pre-Islamic ceremony from the temporal vantage point of the early Islamic period, and to take it for an authentic ritual text would be an anthropological blunder. In fact the poem is at evident pains to avoid transgressing Islamic norms, at least by name. No deity is interpellated so as to imply any particular cultic commitment. But Islamic practice obeys strict constraints where prayer for rain is concerned, and in the ritual described in Wasna's poem (performed in exurban space by an unchaperoned band of women wearing sleeveless garments) those constraints are conspicuously violated.

The ambiguity of Wasna's poem is at its height in verses six and seven, which present the ritual's verbal content. This is where we would look for hymnic material — some simulation of address to a deity, or perhaps repetitive chant. Instead, verses six and seven present as *beggar's speech*, directed at unspecified masculine plural addressees. For these I can supply no precedent in pre-Islamic religious practice. Mortal addressees (passing at night by the camel-wallow?) are even less likely, given the supernatural results of the ritual at the poem's end — namely, the release of rainfall at the direction of a singular "commander" (āmir) in the sky.

The indeterminacy of verses six and seven would seem to be no accident but an intentional "firewall" between the fictional rain-supplication enacted within the poem and any known form of polytheistic devotion, without leaving any doubt in its chronotopic staging outside the ritual world of Islam. (Al-Āmir is not, after all, one of God's ninety-nine Arabic names.) There is only one generation of Arab Muslims for whom such a recollection of pre-Islamic ritual would be imaginable: the generation whose lives spanned the pre-Islamic and Islamic periods. We call this generation the mukhadramūn, and in the history of Arabic poetry they are of huge importance. Wasna's tribe is reported to have adopted Islam in year 11 after the Emigration (= 632 CE); this date may be used to correlate the temporal parameters of the poem. The notional present tense of the poem's performance — its *hinc et nunc* — belongs to the post-11-A.H. Islamic era, while the action it describes dates to the Banu Asad's pre-Islamic days.

So much for the poem's fictive *milieux*. Where to locate the poem in socio-literary history is a harder question. *Contra* Hammond I see nothing internal to the poem that is inharmonious with feminine authorship, but I find no evidence in its favor either. The identity of "Wasna" (attached to this poem only, and in only one source) does little to stabilize things. Her name means "Drowsy-Eyed," and might be understood as a *nomen loquens,* i.e., a name that expresses its bearer's role within some narrative. (*Oedipus,* meaning either "He of the swollen feet" or "He who is known by his feet," is a famous example of this.) *Wasna* is a feminine adjective that derives from *al-wasn,* which is the infinitive form of a verb that means "to nod off," thus defined in the *Book of Rain*: "A well that causes people to lose consciousness is called mūsina, and the fainting spell that people suffer from its water's noxious fumes is called *al-wasn.*" The name Wasna could therefore have emerged from the reminiscence of "wearing out the wells" in the poem's first verse.

For an Islamic-era language artist to adopt the persona of a pre-Islamic poet was not unheard of, and for women singers to set the work of male poets to music was commonplace. There is therefore no place for positivism in the case of the poem's authorship, and (much as I might like to in Kathleen's honor) I am unable to present Wasna to the world as a re-discovered woman poet. Instead, I give to Kathleen Wasna the defiant speaker of the poem, who commemorates the efficacy of women's ritual speech from the already-nostalgic temporal plane of its delegitimization (rhymed in alif-rā', meter: mutaqārib).

WE KNOW YOU SAW US wearing out the wells
        when water kept its distance for too long,
shunning its environs all unjustly
        and reducing our catchpools to arid stone,
when from the crowns of thornèd trees there went up
        in whispers to their lord in Heaven secret cries,
and Earth gaped open to the grievances of camels
        re-echoed in the [empty] water-pits.
At night by the wallow we gathered in desperation.   5
        Our heads were covered and our arms were bare.
"Borrow the right," we said, "to [call your hand]
        a liberal hand, and to the end of your days enjoy
security and freedom! A liberal hand
        may find its gift [to the needy] was but a loan!"
As we braced our insides [for prolonged thirst]
        there lit up a spreading bank of cloud,
and then the cloud advanced, no faster than
        a tender, broken-footed camel drive.
Through portals in its outer edges, it laughed   10
        and sang, and let out stray bursts of tears,
lit up by [lightning] like a lady's sash,
        [rapidly] tied and untied from around her middle.
As we began to doubt [the cloud's] salvation,
        fearing lest it fail to claim our turf,
at a commander's gesture from up above it, [meaning]
        "Let it go," it followed that command.

૮૮૮

SOURCES

I. For Wasna's poem

Anonymous (11th c.?). *Majmu'at al-ma'ani* (A Compilation of Poetic Themes), ed. 'Abd al- Salam Harun (Beirut: Dar al-Jil, 1992), vol. 2, 903-4.

al-'Askari, Abu Hilal. *Diwan al-ma'ani* (A Register of Poetic Themes), ed. Ahmad Hasan Basaj (Beirut: Dar al-Kutub al-'Ilmiyya, 1994), vol. 2, 357.

Ibn Hamdun, Muhammad ibn al-Hasan. *al-Tadhkirat al-Hamduniyya* (Memorabilia of Ibn Hamdun), ed. Ihsan 'Abbas and Bakr 'Abbas (Beirut: Dar Sadir, 1996), vol. 5, 349.

Ibn al-Shajari, Hibat Allah al-Baghdadi. *al-Hamasat al-Shajariyya* (The Thematically Arranged Poetry Anthology of Ibn al-Shajari), ed. 'Abd al-Mu'in Malluhi and Asma' al-Himsi (Damascus: Manshurat Wizarat al-Thaqafa, 1970), vol. 2, 773-6.

al-Khalidiyyan, Abu Bakr Muhammad and Abu 'Uthman Sa'id. *Kitab al-Ashbah wa-'l-naza'ir min ash'ar al-mutaqaddimin wa-'l-jabiliyyati wa-'l-mukhadramin* (The Book of Similarities and Resemblances among the Poetic Works of Early Islam, the Pre-Islamic Period, and the Generation Spanning the Two), ed. al-Sayyid Muhammad Yusuf (Cairo: Lajnat al-Ta'lif wa-'l-Tarjama wa-'l-Nashr, 1958-65), vol. 2, 245-6.

al-Sharif al-Murtada, 'Ali ibn al-Husayn. *Amali al-Murtada: Ghurar al-fawa'id wa-durar al-qala'id* (The Dictations of al-Murtada: Noble Precepts and Necklaced Pearls), ed. Muhammad Abu 'l-Fadl Ibrahim (Cairo: Dar Ihya' al-Kutub al-'Arabiyya/'Isa al-Bab al-Halabi, 1954), vol. 2, 240-1.

II. Secondary Sources

Daqqa, Muhammad 'Ali, ed. *Diwan Bani Asad* (Beirut: Dar Sadir, 1999).

Hammond, Marlé. *Beyond Elegy: Classical Arabic Women's Poetry in Context* (Oxford: Oxford Univ. Press, 2010).

al-Jasim, Ahmad Musa. *Shi'r Bani Asad fi 'l-jahiliyya: Dirasa fanniyya* (Beirut: Dar al-Kunuz al-Adabiyya, 1995).

> *Breaking rules, breaking boundaries, crossing over, going where you've been told not to go . . . . The poem becomes [your]place to break rank[.]*

— Kathleen Fraser, "Line. On the Line."

Influence is mysterious. I would not say that Kathleen Fraser's poetry influenced me. I would say that it has given me myriad possibilities I had not imagined before, that it inspired me. Wait. I think that in fact I'm saying that she influenced me, showed me that I could cross lines, disobey rules. At this point: Allow: wander in order to break rank. Kathleen: *wait for me.*

Poets strive to be "original," yet we also heed the process of *invitation*, *trust*, and *intuitive intertextual engagement* that "influence" entails, as Fraser defined her own relationship to H.D. in a 1996 talk, "The Empty Page: H.D.'s Invitation to Trust and Mistrust Language." She described her "intellectual curiosity," development of a poetics that tracks and investigates process, that challenges and linguistically reforms itself, and how H.D.'s poetry served as an "enspiriting guide." As Fraser remarks about her long palimpsestic sequence, "Etruscan Pages" (1993), for example, "Without H.D.'s precedent, it is very unlikely that I would have trusted my own particular rendering of the clues and layers of the Etruscan culture[.]" Fraser saw a way forward, discovered poetic method and mode, trusted the particular poet that precedent enabled her to be.

When I heard Fraser give this talk, I was embarking on my own particular path — as it happened, the one veering away from the secure insouciance of the able-bodied toward the forcibly embodied constrictions of the chronically ill. I'd lost all markers by which I'd known my world and self, and no longer recognized who I was or where I was going. I felt raw, dumb, and it was in this condition that, all impulsively, I approached Fraser to ask if I might interview her. What was I thinking! Perhaps what I responded to in her *presence* was her personal warmth, for it gave me courage to speak to her. This warmth charges her intellectual and poetic excavations, her open-hearted investigation of world and word, and the far-reaching significance of her multi-faceted contribution to letters. I would come to appreciate the breadth of her particular, poetic journey, Fraser the linguistic explorer, Fraser the path-forger in experimental form, Fraser the Bold Feminist editor as well as poet and essayist. I would also come profoundly to cherish the mentoring hand of friendship she extended, the en-spiriting guide she became for me in my darkest hours. She en-lightened the way forward, which, eventually, I found.

Fraser has spoken about trying to find poetic gestures for recording broken-up time: the self's multiple tracks in the poem, the thought-lines and contrary voices carried within that continuously negotiate and interact with each other. "How marvelous," she has said, "to be able to have one narrative text going, and then to have bits of language to the side that ... locate other, simultaneously held fragments of perception."

Explicity [stet: retain typo]: Explode fragments into the margins of the main text. Create flashes of insight from the accidental. Remain open to error. Make fun of "an attitude of perfection that denies disruption as a reality that denies all the accidents of chance that shape our experience." Break against imagined bindings that feel too tight and get beyond them — even as air does (*boundayr*). [n.b. To *reproduce* error I must correct Word's auto-correct.]

It was — what can I call it but *timely*? — for me to think of the "layers" in Fraser's work, the "bits and pieces of language," my own language a broken and interrupted thing for so long. To write from the embodied experience of chronic illness, I followed Fraser's lead, tracked the "potent" fragments full of insights discovered through or during, despite or even because of, the accidents of verbal eruptions, disruptions. "The fragmented, broken up, interrupted time" out of which women writers have always tried to write — the traces of which Fraser conceptualizes and integrates into her work, rather than attempts to erase — she embraced as an important creative principle. In Fraser's poetry, we can approach these layers archeo/logically, as excavations of levels of socio-cultural experience embedded in and juxtaposed among personal and literary intersections. The creative/formal interactions produce — and are produced by — discovery: flashes of insight often catalyzed by accident. "The accidents/ interest me," Fraser writes:

> She wanted a "flow" she thought, but in the translation
> it was corrected, displacing the *o* and substituting *a*.
> She could give herself to an accident. (*il cuore* 39)

In Fraser's ironic corrective of tradition, "flaw" (as in: displeasing imperfection) displaces "flow" (as in: aesthetically pleasing), and conscious desire is "corrected" not by punishment but by "translation." A typo leads to metaphor and insight, the self-as-gift: an "accident" to which the woman can "give herself."

Invitation, hearing, trust. Fraser's process of trust became a model of poetic attentiveness for me. Here's a beautiful reason why her selected poems, *il cuore: the heart* (1997), closes with one of the most eloquent examples of potent discovery of which I know. Entitled "WING," the final series of poems emerged from what seemed to Fraser to be unconnected levels of social and historical context: the illness and death of a close friend; two exhibits by artist Mel Bochner in Rome (one at the *Museo Storico della Liberazione*) that caused Fraser to ruminate about Italian Fascist and Nazi imprisonment of Jews, Gypsies and resistance fighters during World War II; the archeo/logical remnants of imperial Roman history evident in the architectural layers of Roman walls (becoming Fraser's palimpsestic *arche/text*); and her fascination from childhood with the spiritual iconography of angels and wings. Suddenly the last poem in the series opens to what Fraser has described as error leading to risk and unfettered insight, but I might call, albeit with a bit more magical thinking (*pace* H.D.), *poetic alchemy*. Through an "accident" produced by the formal experimentation that Fraser was conducting, Section X, "Vanishing Point: Third Black Quartet," concretely materialized a *WING*:

```
forward edge itself to be volume by necessity as if partial    erase
edge itself to be volume by necessity as if partial erase    other
itself to be volume by necessity as if partial erase    corners
to be volume by necessity as if partial erase    planes

. . . . . . . . . . . . . . . . . . . . .
by necessity as if partial erase                condensed
necessity as if partial erase                   in

. . . . . . . . . . . . . . . . .
partial erase                     historic
erase                             tendons
```

(*il cuore*, p. 193)

Fraser describes the process of writing this last section as the unplanned, formal re-contextualization of an "out-of-context" experience. An experiment with mechanical/formal repetition leads to a visual discovery (the shape of a wing) and an insight that "being taken outside of my normal frames of reference" catalyzes. As she elaborates in her "Afterword,"

> Isn't the typo, after all, a word trying to escape its
> single-version identity? It wants deciphering. Just as
> the alphabet is 'at large,' so is the fugitive identity of the
> poem . . . on the prowl, looking for its next escape from
> the already known. (*il cuore*, p. 197; Fraser's ellipsis)

Loosening her own approach to language and form from the poetically familiar, the "already known," in order to investigate an accident of stunning visual revelation (*other ways of knowing*, as Fraser once described to me her experiments in visual and hybrid poetics), she breaks boundaries, crosses over into the unknown, the undone, because, as she puts it, *a woman wants to fly.* "WING" spreads its wings, veers into the poetically possible — "itself the wing not static but frayed, layered, fettered, furling."

And unfurling, winging it. Taking us (me) under her wing with her *invitation to trust intuitive intertextual engagement.* And there we are, taking wing. Aloft.

ACKNOWLEDGMENTS

Some portions of this tribute appeared in different form in my earlier critical essay, "'I am not of that feather': Kathleen Fraser's Postmodern Poetics," in *H.D. and Poets After,* ed. Donna Krolik Hollenberg (Iowa City: University of Iowa Press, 2000), pp. 172–83. I've reworked, repatterned, exploded the pieces. Kathleen Fraser's lecture "The Empty Page" was given at the 1996 ALA held in San Diego, later collected in Fraser's essay collection *Translating the Unspeakable: Poetry and the Innovative Necessity* (2000), under the title, "The Blank Page: H.D.'s Invitation to Trust and Mistrust."

Emergency Room, at Haight and Fillmore, The Poetry Center at State, subterranean, by cell-phone light, Athens, Greece, stoops, planes and automobiles, after naps, before naps, in the dark, in a warehouse, in the classroom first, before bed, first thing in the morning, bootlegged VHS, Dolores Park, second-hand books, Susan Gevirtz, Peter Weltner, Steve Dickison, scarves, San Francisco, the household, the NET Outtakes, "she lives part of each year in Italy," Kathleen Fraser, New York, 1964, dinners, Molotov's on a Saturday afternoon, the SF International Poetry Festival, texting Susan Gevirtz late one night in 2014 "Lying in bed reading Kathleen Fraser's *Translating the Unspeakable*; just what I needed, can't put it down, fully energized, I love her poetry, first time reading her poetics/memoir, in love all over again," hieroglyphics/pictographs, BOUNDAYR BOUNDARY, !!!, the Etruscans, the San Franciscans, the fog, the sun

A little Kathleen Fraser free association; looking at that list I seem to be traveling a lot with Kathleen, strange locations, modes of transportation, times of day, the qualities of light San Francisco manifests, tactile memories and moods emerge; arcana (the story of how Kathleen rescued the NET Outtakes footage from a KQED dumpster, unbelievable, mythical to us SFSU undergrads), a poetics, the history, the grace, the politics that Kathleen represents and conjures.

Kathleen Fraser was my ur-poet.

In 2001 I read her *il cuore: the heart*, this set it all off

from re:searches

not random, these
crystalline structures, these
non-reversible orders, this
camera forming tendencies, this
edge of greater length, this
lyric forever error, this

something embarrassingly clear, this
　　　language we come up against

we come up against this language, not random, these poems, these people,
this syntax is a way of being, this singular embarrassing art, this Kathleen
Fraser, this hero and her art, feeding the rest of us, I can travel with her
in this city, in this light and dark thing, how many years ago did I read
her and think, yes I Am Home, a boundary redefined, a place where,
BOUNDAYR, we meet at the line, the mistake, the syntax, the air we
breath, I Am Home here, in the error, thank you Kathleen.

As if a letter

an *a*

the memory of beginning
or beginning again
the torn half-obliterated *a* of the cover   the whole need to remember   (the
memory in the very muscles of the hand, the arm, learning how to write,
bending the pencil to one's own will, the *word*, spelling
spelling it
coaxing it
hexing it

spelling (a spell)

The cover to uncover **TYYPE**   "**movable**"
the history of typography   the metaphor ::: glancing toward
Gutenberg

the infinite ways not to spell

Kathleen's non-narrative

magicked

§§§

*& ghosts   mysterious disappearances   faux noir
clues   the clue of the "missing nightgown"*

An unstable narrator she chases (chastens)
the spectator   again a false ending   a
comedy   a marriage made among the stars

She displays great generosity in her willingness to attempt the translation
of paintings into language; language that evades outright and obvious
"description," that regards chance and the tangential as elements of
composition:

> *"she explores how any particular work*
>
> is altered by
> its placement how any
> discrete figure apart
> from the bottom half of
> its body ..."

and so on, imagining the change of figure or attitude or pose or additions
of other features in the painting: a window or a door, another angle
of light. The painting is an object, but in Kathleen's eyes it is possibly
unfinished, an object one sees into, moves closer to, observes aside from
the representational, *paint* with all its
peculiarities, as laid down by the artist whose work itself is subtly
changed by its exposure to the world.

hi dde violeth i dde violet

an experiment in splitting words " (fis s **ion**) " from which we learn
that split words like split atoms explode with energy. This poem may be a
new *gnosis*, a modern Gnostic Gospel, an absurdist gospel. Imagine Our

Lady hurling *mozzarella* "in equal prts" & "violet" becomes "violent." Perhaps, as Terry Eagleton has proposed, the root of religion is *terror*.

It is a poem of huge range, spanning everyday mundaneness, (coffee & eggs, *Easter eggs*) with pages representing yelling, howling, which suggests the pagan origins of Easter, the "rites of spring," the beauty & incredibility of Christ's resurrection. "He arose" but finally he is a rose, the bloom of both mortal and eternal life, the rose celebrated in countless rose windows in as many cathedrals in Western civilization.
The punning of a line like "...no longer roll'd awry" might very well seem blasphemous to a believing Christian, but those of us who loved the poetry of the King James translation of the Bible will take pleasure in this comic rendition of the scene in Gesthemane. One, after all, loved the poetry more than the story or its moral.

Second Language

One wants to think into childhood   the way it was in summer
And that's where it was   all cut up we had a text   we cut into shreds and rearranged on a page   the way we made scrapbooks then   pretty ladies dressed in blue

And the grasshoppers, "husks of dead locusts"   the summer part of swimming and shade and bug bites   Then school

> *first day.*

> *window shadow*
> *just as grown-ups look into*

> *their passed sheets of*
> *right words*

Language *is* a second language   always replacing whatever came before, the language of angels perhaps, or of lambs, the beloved animals of childhood. All that given over for the

right words

the words we are taught to say, to read: school as a social control, as the institution which molds us, teaches us conformity — but Kathleen's poem looks to the margins, to the places where play is still possible.

There is more, always more, but I will quote the final page of this section:

second language

from laying down
the bend of certainty

you sound [dwell] in one
word enough

resistant to a fact that can
refuse fumbling

I want to thank Kathleen for her tribute to John Coltrane, whose rendition of "My Favorite Things" means something like *the morning of the world* to me.

November 20th, 2014

It was one of those ideas. We have had so many, together and apart. Well, especially Kathleen and JoAnn. Small unlikely plots that usher from innocent cappuccinos drunk happily just off major piazzas. Something about the visual and literary imaginations that bond to strong coffee.

Don and Arthur, of course, give their assent as a direct result of a kind of gin logic. It was an autumn idea. There was that first bite. The north wind, blowing clear and cold, full of the optimism of new seasons with their flurry of color.

One day JoAnn says she and Kathleen had decided to abandon the usual Thanksgiving. The guest list evaporated like the dark autumn mist. It wasn't exactly rebellion, although there was a rebellious component. It was an idea, sprung fully formed. At first it didn't even seem possible. We would celebrate the season in the backyard. Just the four of us. A pilgrim's pilgrimage in reverse.

No table groaning with the familiar excesses. No fraught seating arrangements, no rented table and chairs. Just a classic autumn dinner outside in the late afternoon. And it was sweet. Conversation about poetry and art and a little logic. Soft voices amid bare roses, a drift of liquid amber leaves. It was also cold. Heavy-coat cold. *Al fresco* shading toward *al freddo*.

But so consistent. It starts in 1968 in George Hitchcock's Laguna Street house. Kathleen and Don were Kayak irregulars helping George put the magazine together in exchange for salami and cheap beer. A year later Don printed *Sawdark,* Kathleen's magazine from SF State. Years pass in parallel poetic universes, Kathleen running The Poetry Center at State and Don the West Coast Print Center in Berkeley. Time passes until 1982, when JoAnn's nude drawing appears on a wonderful broadside of Kathleen's poem, *Interior with Madame Vuillard and Son,* at a Stanford show of women's work. Soon after, JoAnn and Don show up in Rome where Kathleen and Arthur have a lovely apartment and the "Salon Years" ensue. There are shared dinners, paintings, drawings, plays, philosophy, poems. There are Rome walks, museum crawls, movies, restaurants. There are JoAnn and Kathleen's collaborations, including *Second Language,* the result of long working days at their shared studio at the American Academy.

All, however, is prefigured by the Thanksgiving in the garden. Icons and iconoclasm. Humor in the service of deep seriousness. Art punctuated by good food and wine. Our mutual artistic lives fed over and over with the generosity engendered by decades of friendship, or more simply, love.

Drawing: JoAnn Ugolini

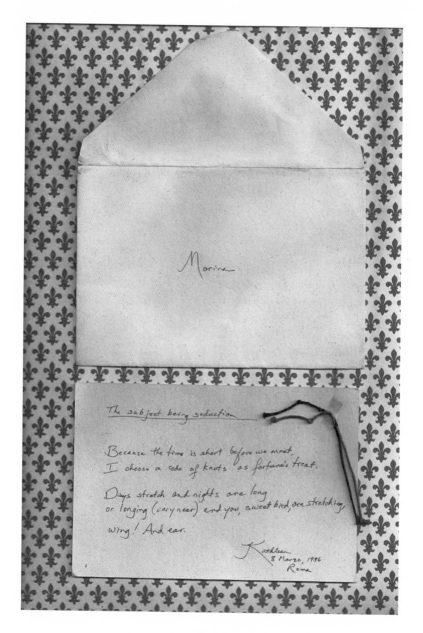

On March 8th, 1996, Kathleen and I were to meet at our favorite winebar, called "Semidivino" (a polysemous word in itself: it means "half-divine", but when read as a string of three words, it also means "seeds of wine"; obviously, the pun was intentional,) to celebrate International Women's Day.

Kathleen was a bit late, which was not unusual, but probably a good thing, in the end: the short wait gave me just the right time to mentally prepare for her appearance, because meeting Kathleen was no ordinary event; something special would always happen when I was around her. The alchemy, this time, was tied to a red thread, a *fil rouge* which was harmoniously and intriguingly intertwined with a black thread, as in the picture above.

Kathleen had written the poem and made this card especially for me, and for the transition that I was going through at that time. It was a period of personal growth, both intellectual and existential (after my first marriage ended I had met my new love, the marvelous man who is still by my side). Kathleen, also called Caterina when in Rome, was sharing in my happiness, and, as typical of her, playing in a sophisticated way with the idea of "seduction," which she compared to the stretching of a new powerful "wing," able to soar higher and higher. It was March 8th, and we were both in a playful mood. Kathleen had chosen that "code of knots" as "fortune's treat," and her welcoming of the new stretching of "wing," and of "ear," as a new universe of pleasure was starting to replace all my fears.

There is a *fil rouge* or common thread which runs through my more-than-two-decade-long friendship with Kathleen Fraser. And the thread is obviously poetry, but also a broader notion of creation attached to it. Kathleen is the one who, somehow, made me who I am today, enhancing my creativity and trusting my potential talent as a translator of poetry, always supporting my projects, dreams and daring flights in the field of literature. No words to express my eternal gratitude will ever suffice; my feelings towards her are imbued with this constant impulse of gratitude.

From the Nineties up to the present day, Kathleen has represented a guide and an inspiration to me where poetry is concerned. As recently as last month she wrote a compelling piece of autobiographical criticism for the Forum on Voices of American Experimental Poetry which I coordinated for the journal of American Studies in Italy, *RSA*. The issue will be soon out, and her voice is pivotal. Not only did Kathleen contribute to the Forum by generously giving me her piece, but, most importantly, her work represented the crux of my discourse; she has pitched in with her suggestions since the project began. Kathleen never discourages you, even when you are evidently confused or doubtful, or unfocused; instead, she teaches you how to find resources within yourself — self-criticism, self-confidence, trust, vision, and balance to change direction and find your true path. In my own career, Kathleen represents the red arrow pointing to the *core* of my mind.

I have translated various poems by Kathleen, but primarily I worked on her *Etruscan Pages* (2001), witnessing the conception and development of the longish composition as it took shape. Another "red thread" which links us to one another:

The two colors mentioned above, red and black, are a leitmotif in Etruscan painting, and they are conceived as a chromatic dance, "little sentences freely written in red paint or black," as if to represent a harmoniously resolved enigma, in their symmetry and mirroring balance, and this resembles what translation is, at its best. This, among other crucial things, is what I learned from Kathleen.

One of the finest fibers intertwined in the common thread which binds me to Kathleen is made up of the many occasions I had to explore issues involved in translating poetry during our ongoing dialogue devoted to this subject, as she discussed her writings and her compositional procedures.

wind sifts iron filings'
carelessly drawn script

downhill writing
carved with metal object

or red and black brushed with finger
into soft stone recess

above the place they lay the dead one

.

we know what each mark is equal to
but not, in retrospect, what was intended

.

wanting messages, "little sentences
freely written in red paint or black"

↓↑ƧИꓸ
ΟϿ∧ИꝹ

During the lengthy sessions of exegetical debate which accompanied our meetings and conversations over the years — talks with the author that enabled me to disclose the multi-layered meaning of her poetry more authentically and render it in Italian in a more comprehensive fashion — I can clearly identify a number of "epiphanies" in the process of my analysis of the aforementioned *Etruscan Pages* (2001), but also *Notes Preceding Trust* (1987).

For instance, from the latter collection, consider the following quote from the piece entitled "re-searches":

> not random, these
> crystalline structures, these
> non reversible orders, this
> edge of greater length, this
> lyric forever error, this
> something embarrassingly clear, this
> language we come up against.

These lines perfectly describe the awareness that poetry, translation and composition do overlap in a single instance of creation, where the direction and pace are determined and provided by language itself, in the process of its making in the poet's mind and on the page.

In "Giotto: ARENA," from the collection *when new time folds up* (1993), Kathleen Fraser hints at the painter's perfect "circle," made "'Not by system, but by / wrist,' / G. said, / substituting body parts," where the artistic endeavor is compared to a bodily act, corresponding to the dynamic gesture of creation. It is a gesture which somehow replicates the mechanics and articulation of a bird's flight:

> Attached by some 'natural' substance
> the arm (or leg) with elbow

(or joint) midway suggests the next
incision or protrusion: It stiffens as

a fin or rib projecting new function:

It emits signals periscopic (familiar) helical into the spinal: Wing

could loosen that line's identity calling
to itself with charcoal error

'only in contradiction to that which is known
to us of nature'

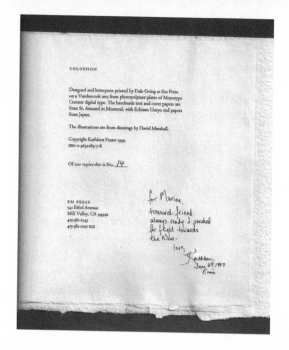

COLOPHON

Designed and letterpress printed by Dale Going at Em Press
on a Vandercook 325 from photopolymer plates of Monotype
Centaur digital type. The handmade text and cover papers are
from St. Amand in Montreal, with Echizen Unryu end papers
from Japan.

The illustrations are from drawings by David Marshall.

Copyright Kathleen Fraser 1995.
ISBN 0-9632085-7-8

Of 200 copies this is No. _14_

EM PRESS
541 Ethel Avenue
Mill Valley, CA 94941
415-381-1243
415-381-0130 FAX

for Marine,
treasured friend
always ready & parched
for flight towards
the New.
love,
Kathleen
June 29/1997
Roma

The evocation of a wing — with all the symbolic as well as physical references associated with it — is a perfect metaphor for the essential function of translation, and, *a priori* and along with that, of *w(rit)ing.*

The notion of "writing" has the suggestion of the force of a "wing" built into it: w(rit)ing, and Kathleen has always encouraged me — as well as the hundreds of followers/admirers/students fortunate enough to have her as tutor during her creative-writing courses at San Francisco University — to undertake even loftier challenges, turning distance into fusion, blending differences to form a whole, and making of them understanding. Consider her book *Discrete Categories Forced into Coupling* (2004), a masterful example of "the intellectual and elusively sensate aspects of visual and literary aesthetic connection" (Carla Harryman), and a work whose filiform texture (or, to use the author's own expression, "grains of rice") affords a concentration of existence: the capillary tissue and intricate fabric of reality is filtered through an intensified consciousness directed inwards, and this infinitesimal intensity of perception leads to a rare — albeit rarified — act of being. "Deceptively quiet in manner, its intimate foci and tone make clear the ground of our contemporary lives, our 'being together' despite the distances of isolating thought" (Robert Creeley). Kathleen's poetry reestablishes the foundations of our existence, making it self-evident that we can only construct that existence on intangibility and elusiveness.

I've understood, too, that writing on a lined page, particularly within the covers of a notebook, has provided me with a landscape of continuous blue horizons, below which I can sink, above which I may again rise, so that each line extended and wrapped into the next enacts a kind of hope, a proof that life below the horizontal does exist and may arise of its own motion or impetus to continue, as in breath, over which we have little control, although we can learn procedures, directing it to foreign anatomical regions. (Kathleen Fraser, *Discrete Categories Forced into Coupling*, 2004, p. 19)

In my essay "Translation and the (re)location of the poetical surface: Kathleen Fraser's *exemplum*" (2007), I ventured the hypothesis that Fraser's compositional procedures resemble the process of translation. That is to say, through the act of translation we can achieve an understanding of the process of the composition of her poetry — as was the case with the other experimental poets whom I happened to translate (here I'm referring primarily to Gertrude Stein, Charles Olson, and Robert Creeley). It is then, perhaps, not a coincidence that Kathleen's collection of essays is entitled *Translating the Unspeakable: Poetry and the Innovative Necessity* (2000). In her "How Did Emma Slide? A Matter of Gestation" (1979) Kathleen confesses: "The writing wanted to reflect what was turning out to be a painful breaking-down process," which beautifully dovetails with the translator's craft, always negotiating between what is said and what's left unsaid. In *Etruscan Pages* once again, referring to the inscriptions carved on the rocky surface of the ancient necropolis, Kathleen is obviously intrigued and enthralled by the mystery of the Etruscan language: "'we know what each mark is equal to, but in retrospect...' // red paint or black," and later,

> Was A
> Where
> you made and
> unmade your mind...
>
> first hesitation
>
> when you doubted
> what you
> thought you
> were
> looking for?

I consider this common thread of always "looking for" a meaning in words/through words- and looking for "others"/ "the other"/ "otherness" in words — to be an unbreakable bond of affection, devotion, and admiration which inextricably binds me — with a *fil rouge* — to the poet Kathleen Fraser.

Rome, January 9th, 2015

Kathleen Fraser
Lunch Poems, October 18th, 2012
Morrison Library, UC Berkeley

Kathleen Fraser was introduced beautifully by Robert Hass and then gave a full, deep, resonant retrospective reading, from work written in the mid-1980s to the present, which was then 2012. At one point, she was talking about one of her artists' books, *S E C O N D Language*, a collaborative work with JoAnn Ugolini, and showing the pages to the audience, saying how much she admired her friend JoAnn's collages, and wanted to — and DID — cut up one of her pieces, a memoir that hadn't been published, to make these poems. So, a gorgeous visual collage on the left-hand side, a sumptuous verbal collage on the right side. It's this work by Kathleen that I chose to present here: I took some of her words from a section of *S E C O N D Language* and moved them around. The release she found when making that work, I found when taking the found words and forming them into two-word lines, two-line stanzas.

From Kathleen Fraser's *S E C O N D Language*, a Third

Breathe morning
In day

The beginning
Measuring how

Photo night
Like shadow

Outlining bones
The dark

Edges green
Oars red

Husks in day
Down they

Go how
The stars

Could start
I saw

Letters large
And full

Use time
Little pencils

As background
Measuring morning

Being just
Wet paper

Words on
Shirt cardboards

December 6th, 2014

"I want to write you as soon as possible…"

A clearing   "took possession of me"   on the page

                                                        "I began to hear
                                                        and to give value
                                                        to my own interior"

                                        ⟨⟨⟨

Life took me (her) you   on an unreliable path/
                                              looking for something
                                              "partial not yet arrived"

            so as to break free
                        from pre-made
                                emotional/intellectual parameters

                                        ⟨⟨⟨

                                deviation the
                                vied for
                                glitch
                                in the itch

∭

There where blunder
        moved her body ~~in a certain~~ to an
      uncertain
         position

in the utterance
         would lead
         Her, She, I
                 to fall into
                       Her, She, I

∭

"how errors began to appear"

stumbling into the ~~beautiful~~ "simplicity" of it

a transgression
of sorts
in color

wander   rrrrrrrrrrrrrrrring
"hello"
intrigued by the language
you know what I mean?

We both said/wrote it

The entire page
remembers her history
                   of an alternate vision

    real concerns of

               other, and "the shaping hand of influence"
               rising to the surface

Here

in the breeze

"... take the risk of being a sender..."

⁂

Working note: "...a poetics of sufficient depth and complexity...."

She has her books out on the table, reads a poem, reads her notes, reads wingtips and reads. She is writing something on Kathleen, for Kathleen. How does one write for or on another without turning it all into a flag, flapping about loosely, in the breeze. But she has a history with her that began as a student, turned into a wave, continued as a friend, in San Francisco, New York, Paris — the ways that lives in poetry intersect, grow deeper because of reading the other on a lake, in the foreground — because of mutual acquaintances, because of respect and admiration. She works through her notes, her emblems, her... waiting for, the oxygen — one of the ones who gave/claimed possibility, permission (at a desk). And a clearing, for error, for mapping the changes (as she once said). Also wanting to say, she was curious (pleasure in her blue eyes). And the world is.... She questions, writes, foregrounds correspondence, includes "states of uncertainty," travels the space of the page, colors it.

§§§

And symmetry?   the "struggle to be human"

"After months of starting and stopping,"
                              glide, slide, then the up-draft

Swan dive

As I flew forward and backward

until

something
turned error   into pleasure

(*All quoted material is by Kathleen Fraser*)

I met Kathleen sometime around 1990, when I was a graduate student at UCLA, trying to find my intellectual way. Among other qualities I love about Kathleen is her generosity, companion to her unflagging energy. She embraced me when I wrote (pre-email, at least for me) to ask if I could speak to her about *HOW(ever)*. The postcard she sent back opened with characteristic élan: "O Elisabeth!" she exclaimed, and I traveled from LA to San Francisco to join her for coffee in North Beach. In the years that followed, Kathleen mentored me, introduced me to other women scholars/writers ("you *need* to know her," she would say — always right), and helped me to read her work and that of many other poets I was only then discovering. How can I describe Kathleen's profound influence on my work, my thinking, what I care about? She has been my guide since I first read her and met her. To celebrate Kathleen, I decided to cite her. Doing so gives me great joy. Knowing Kathleen—reading, rereading Kathleen—gives me even more.

CENTO (from Kathleen... *for* Kathleen)

> *It turned out that there* were *a few women writing poetry*
> —"The Tradition of Marginality"

                                   from that edge or brink or borderline
                  something travels circuitously and we give over
the blank page

                             walking touched
we entered the room, we were still small
                 observed from triangular pouches rising beneath the ungovernable
                                      we felt unfamilied, without a *place*
                                     a fin or rib projecting new function:
as if each dream or occasion of pain had tried to lift itself

grief is simple and dark

an addendum

what you'll refer to. A dream of separate rooms

only in contradiction to that which is known

It turned out that there *were* a few women writing poetry

the New comes forward in its edges in order to be itself

something you meant to teach yourself to remember

you begin from anywhere, nowhere. Language is a private tryst

the letter A is a plow

light forgetting itself   light falling loosely

(this boundary you make up in your mind)

but we want a record of us where there is "nothing"

the authority of her task, returned to her

itself the wing not static but frayed, layered, fettered, furling

rooms carved with tool

and cells as if by other names did call

wingspans slap and break loose in the hot dust

death imagines us into pleasure. We want to continue

It turned out that there *were* a few women writing poetry

these experiments may be modified to infinity

SOURCES

"The Tradition of Marginality"
"Four voices telling stories about light and dark"
WING
"from Fiamma's Sketchbook"
"Etruscan Pages"
"Somebody who is hooked on the color red"
"You can hear her breathing in the photograph"
"The Uncontainable"
"Locations"
when new time folds up
"1930"
"'La La at the Cirque Fernando, Paris'"

> *This is my letter to the World*
> — Emily Dickinson

> *I confuse you with the reader. The love poem is always addressed to you.*
> — Steve Benson, "Echo"

Dear Readers:

I started this piece on Kathleen Fraser's work as an essay, but its subject is the letter as a formal strategy, so why not write one? As soon as I addressed you, the writing's tone shifted, became more intimate and playful, less formal. What happens when an interlocutor appears, even a disembodied one?

   The letter as a formal strategy has a venerable literary history. It is even older than I imagined. Ovid's *Heroides* is epistolary, as are Chaucer's short poems "which imagine themselves… as letters to an addressee" (Horvath). Horace's *Ars Poetica*, his treatise on the art of poetry, is composed in verse as a letter to Lucius Calpurnius Piso. Poetry has a long and ongoing relationship with the epistolary. We can't forget the many delicious epistolary novels appearing in the 18th century, including Samuel Richardson's *Pamela* and *Clarissa*, and Choderlos de Laclos's *Les Liaisons Dangereuses*.

   These novels are highly gendered, with male authors ventriloquizing female characters whose correspondence is presented as found, authentic documents. Come to think about it, Ovid's *Heroides* too is highly gendered, most of its epistolary poems written in the voice of epic heroines — Penelope, Dido, Phaedra, etc. Some of these letter poems demand redress.

   Penelope to the tardy Ulysses:
            do not answer these lines, but come, for
   Troy is dead and the daughters of Greece rejoice.

   But all of Troy and Priam himself
   are not worth the price I've paid for victory.

With some writers in particular, it is generative and a joy to read their poetry alongside their letters, or their letters alongside their poetry, perhaps because both forms — poem and letter — are particularly imbricated, for example, in the work of George Oppen and Emily Dickinson. Plenty of contemporary innovative writers have found the letter a generous and capacious form: in Nate Mackey's hands "N" writes to the Angel of Dust, while Jack Spicer speaks to Garcia Lorca, and Dodie Bellamy's Mina Harker addresses the reader, Dr. Van Helsing, Sam, Sing, and others. There is often something sexy in this address. Don't you think? A siren call.

As I've been rereading Kathleen Fraser's work, I've been struck by the letter's recurring presence across the body of her writing. What does Kathleen do with this form?

"this. notes. new year," published in Fraser's book *Each Next* in 1980,[1] is a poem in prose blocks that begins:

> Dear other, I address you in sentences. I need your nods
> and I hear your echoes. There is forward movement
> still, as each word is a precedent for what new order.

Here the addressee, the "other," appears as an imagined interlocutor, or maybe it is the community of poetry readers that is hailed and then they — their attention — provides a means for moving forward into the writing in a "new year," full of possibility, with language offering opportunities for "what new order." While the poem is addressed, it isn't signed. Yet, like all letters, it is dialogical (an exchange), perspectival (its structure and content shifting with the recipient and the passage of time) and emergent (not strictly structured but variable and contingent) (Stanley).

Traversing the domestic ("the sound of a low gas flame" and "Christmas is over and 'I'm glad,' I said to David"), Fraser's letter also inscribes the writer's wrestling with the poetic, political, and intellectual provocations made by language poetry and Ron Silliman's "new sentence" in the Bay Area circa 1980:

> One man said of another that he was committed to the
> sentence. I sentence you. I could hear the terseness of
> his sentences and how seductive it seemed to move the
> words always towards a drop in the voice. What did
> it mean to be flat? Was there a principle of denial? Of
> manipulation? I'm worried. He is embarrassed.

Thus, the letter records the social and poetic landscape of the present, or what will become, history. The writer who pens the epistolary poem expresses worry and unfurls a series of questions occasioned by considering the "commit[ment] to the sentence."

Yet the speaker of the poem finds herself "released into sentences." These sentences, while sometimes paratactic, are invested in affect. Addressing her interlocutor again, near the end of the poem, the writer asserts,

> You are against confession, because it's embarrassing.
> I want to embarrass you. To feel your confusion.
> Someone's rhythm sneaking in again. Sharing a
> language. The osmosis of rubbing up. Communing.

In its intimate address, Kathleen's epistolary carries with it the second-person point of view; it courts confession, embarrassment, cites cell biology and chemistry in "osmosis," which, it is worth recalling, is about equalizing "the concentrations on either side of the membrane." It brings the body into it, proposes sharing ideas, feelings, and in its echo of communion, suggests something spiritual.

Letters, it turns out, keep recurring. In "Etruscan Pages" from the book *when new time folds up* (1993), Fraser includes two letters in the midst of a poem that is lineated and in some sections employs stanzas, and incorporates graphic elements (another facet of Kathleen's work that proliferates over the course of her career). The second letter, addressed to Susan (probably Susan Gevirtz who had travelled with

Fraser to Italy), quotes Wallace Stevens in "On Poetic Truth," asserting that "an isolated fact, cut loose from the universe, has no significance for the poet. It derives its significance from the reality to which it belongs." Fraser's citation of Stevens in a letter to her friend and fellow poet written on June 18th, 1991, continues, among other things, to note an ongoing thinking-through and experimentation with how sentences — paratactic and hypotactic — work and what they have to do with the project of poetry for a writer "wanting messages, 'little sentences.'" The Stevens quote also reverberates with the poem's subject matter — the Etruscans — and the fact that what remains of this culture is fragmentary and conjectural, given there is little of Etruscan writing extant and even less that is decipherable. "Etruscan Pages" explains that across a message before a tomb, someone has "inscribed with the hidden / particularity of one still alive / I am Larthia." This female name, overwritten on top of a previous text at the site of a tomb, marks a proto-feminist intervention, feminism a concern to which the poetry and letters-within-poems consistently return.

For example, "this. note" also marks the emergent interest in the late Seventies and early Eighties among a number of women writers and intellectuals in the work of French feminist writers — Irigaray, Cixous, Kristeva: "I wanted, suddenly, to speak French because of certain French women thinking about layers, thinking in layers. But as yet not translated."

The letters in "Etruscan Pages" in their address to friends and fellow writers configure intimacy; they make commune with others, in thoughtful, desirous conversation.

Fraser uses the letter form to probe social and literary politics and their relation to feminism and friendship in "Notes re: Echo," also from *Each Next*. This poem is comprised of dated prose sections that sometimes read like journal entries, within which are interspersed two letters composed by "Echo," addressed to "Dear Narcissus." Dedicated to Steve Benson, Fraser's poem uses the letter to formulate questions of language and sentences: "is language, in fact, the pool?" and "It was, of course, a question of language." Echo writes to Narcissus that "I missed our talks, which always pull me somewhere new, but in your friendly red wagon with its creaky wheels" — signaling the pair's friendship and the centrality of their "talks" that, while challenging, are also safe. However, in Narcissus's absence, when she is alone, Echo begins composing

> stories [that] were written within a solid and digested tradition of linked sentences. Achieving their life gave me a kind of satisfaction I'd not known.

Here, Echo is not pulled along by Narcissus's concerns, not condemned to repeat, as she is in the myth, what Narcissus speaks, but finds herself pursuing her own writerly pleasures, though are these too a kind of echo, the echo of "digested tradition"? Is there pleasure in an echo? The poem plumbs these questions. At the same time, Fraser's poem is in conversation with Steve Benson's piece "Echo," a performance of which she probably attended in 1981.[2] Benson's "Echo" involves two voices (male in the recording from 1986 available at PennSound[3]) reading sentences that unfold seemingly via loose association, with the speakers taking turns "echoing," one another with variable and exquisitely calibrated modulation, including for example, the sentence, "You are really gone" and "The echo is blunt-eared," lines that Fraser in turn echoes by inserting them in "Notes re: Echo.

A complex gender and poetic politics underlies Fraser's poem, part of which explores how the speaker will construct herself through clothing and discourse as she tries on various scenarios for the first class of the semester, and then the poem delineates a conversation among three women, two students and teacher:

> 'What makes you most anxious about this class?'

> One woman wrote, "I am afraid that what I want to say will not be important enough."

> On reading this statement, another woman remarked: "You could drop that part. We're really beyond that.

Interestingly, though Narcissus does not speak in this poem, we find women too have difficulty listening and are given to echoing not only another's speech but also ideology; simultaneously, once again, the poem seems to trace the dynamic and provocative arrival of "language writing" on the poetry scenes in the Bay Area. Letters are, thus, not simply a record of a single individual's intimate or intellectual life, but a site for enacting, deliberating and elaborating an *ars poetica*, a theorizing in *media res* of what one is attempting, enacting; Fraser's epistolary poems make material the fact that, as Montaigne claimed, "friendship feeds on communication," so too, does poetry.

Notes Preceding Trust (1987) includes a poem that is comprised entirely of letters: "Five letters from one window, San Gimignano, May 1981." The poems appear with time notations: "Dear Michael" at 4pm, "Dear Steve" at 4:30pm, "Dear Sue" at 5:30pm, "Dear Andrea" at 6:18, and "Dear Bob" at 7:39. Once again, these letters are addressed but unsigned; the room, the desk and the window before it where the writer sits make a frame for each composition. A bee appears, is covered with an overturned glass, and later released. The writer inquires whether Susan is "happier, now," comments on a story written by Bob: "One of the things that attracts me about the story you just sent me is the way you begin with the end of a thread and wind it as you go." To Steve, she writes, "In the presence of such history, the urge to be original diminishes." She asks of Andrea:

> But why deny this partialness as part of our writing?
> Why not find formal ways to visually articulate its
> complexity — the ongoing secret life — without
> necessarily making it a candidate for the simple-
> minded "confessional"? Writing is, in part, a record
> of our struggle to be human, as well as our delight in
> reimagining/reconstructing the formal designs and
> boundaries of what we've been given.

Perhaps the letter enables the intimacy of the lyric, a space to address
— the beloved, the reader, the fellow writer, the friend — in a moment
of the present, soon to disappear or become history, a space-time place
where one's feeling, as Frank O'Hara said, as well as one's thoughts in
conversation might be remembered, "turned into history," even as the
old forms — the lyric, the "simple confessional" — have become tainted
with solipsism and are inadequate for the challenge under pen. Kathleen's
letters are all ears. Their ethos is as much about listening, relation,
community, questioning, attempting as it is about declaring the writer's
presence, tracing a poetics as it happens. The letters turn to and are
addressed to the world, and that includes us.

With gratitude and appreciation—
Robin

1. All references to Fraser's poems refer to *il cuore*.
2. See Fraser's "Partial local coherence: Regions with illustrations (Some notes on
'Language' Writing)" in *Translating the Unspeakable: Poetry and Innovative Necessity*
(Tuscaloosa: The University of Alabama Press, 2000), pp. 63-76.
3. See: https://media.sas.upenn.edu/pennsound/authors/Benson/10-27-86/Benson-
Steve_04_Echo_EyeMediae_Ann-Arbor_MI_10-27-86.mp3

WORKS CITED

Benson, Steve, "Echo," Reading at Eye Mediae, Ann Arbor MI, October 27, 1986.
PennSound: Center for Programs on Contemporary Writing, University of Pennsylvania,
Web.

Dickinson, Emily, "This is my letter to the world," *The Complete Poems of Emily
Dickinson*, ed. Thomas H. Johnson (Boston: Little Brown and Company, 2010).

Fraser, Kathleen, *il cuore: the heart — Selected Poems 1970–1995* (Hanover, NH: Wesleyan University Press, 1997).

Horvath, Richard P., "Chaucer's Epistolary Poetic: The Envoys to Bukton and Scogan," *The Chaucer Review* 37.2 (2002).

Montaigne, Michel, *The Complete Essays of Montaigne*, trans. Donald Frame (Stanford, CA: Stanford University Press, 2000).

O'Hara, Frank, "In Memory of My Feelings," *The Selected Poems of Frank O'Hara*, ed. Donald Allen (New York: Vintage Books, 1974).

Ovid, *Heroides*, trans. Harold Isbell (New York: Penguin Books, 2004).

Stanley, Liz, "The Epistolarium: On Theorizing Letters and Correspondences," *Auto/Biography* 12 (2004), pp. 201-35.

Dear Kathleen,

You came forward to greet me some thirty years ago, when you were just beginning *HOW(ever)* and I was translating French feminist writers with one hand and piecing together Mina Loy's life with the other. Our meeting was a godsend.

Until that point it had felt as if no one else understood the connections between the modernist women of Loy's day and our own investigations into the possibilities of a *parler-femme*, to borrow from Irigaray. Your recognition of what women like her were doing in and about language, of their work's generative power, and your welcoming me to speak about these things in your SF State poetry course, made all the difference to me in the years after my move from Paris to California. You welcomed me into a flourishing literary milieu and a friendship that led to much delightful cavorting, sometimes in places like New York, Rome, and Paris.

Thinking back to those early days I am moved by your kindness in inviting me to join the *HOW(ever)* collective, along with Frances Jaffer and Beverley Dahlen, then Rachel Blau DuPlessis and Susan Gevirtz. Our collaborations brought me into a network of vital exchanges about present-day poetics and our rapport with foremothers (the term of the day) like H.D., Stein, Riding, Richardson, and Loy.

Thank you too for your rare generosity in the years when I was writing *Becoming Modern*, my biography of Loy, especially for your deeply thoughtful reading of the manuscript. Since then you have often refreshed my spirits while helping me remain alert to our shared perception of modernity, and to "our want to locate that, structurally, in the look and sound of our writing" (to borrow from you!). I so much admire and appreciate the wit, courage and inventiveness with which your poems and essays delineate a door that opens onto an unbounded space where we can locate ourselves.

Kathleen, in writing to you now, I've understood that it was this spaciousness of vision that made possible my fleeting return to poetry

— inspired by a statue in a graveyard and by the "corners, planes and/accumulated depth" of your magnificent *WING*.

Merci mille fois, my dear friend.

ONE WINTER MORNING WE MEET
THE ANGEL. By chance. Or by design. Her
gaze is cast down, her plumage unfurled. She speaks of love,
mobility, power. Imperious in her grace, she resembles us. A spirit
made of flesh, this messenger has passed from heaven to earth —
where she remains. With us, among us. Her back, her unprotected
part, speaks mutely of damage. Like us, she has known gravity
and pain. She is air become stone become woman, her flights
sequential transits, transformations. She bears a blessing. She is
the body of love transfigured in the world, not beyond it. In the
cold graveyard, where other wings enfold eons of sleep, her
feathers (fetters?) lift, open. We turn, she casts her soul into the air.

Today, I was driving to Brewer and back to Ellsworth listening to a radio show from a couple years ago in which one New York psychoanalyst interviewed another, and one of them said that a leader is a leader because such a person goes "out on a limb," and this makes that person "credible" to others. "Credible" seemed to mean that the person has some kind of personal presence, courage, risk, resulting in an accountability and stature that, for others, might lead to their seeing a way that they might believe could be taken, consequently. It happens when you know from the proof of such a stretch as a leader may venture to make who's there behind the positions and the ideas that she articulates, espouses or critiques.

A couple months earlier, I was driving somewhere else listening to Kathleen Fraser's talk of June 6th, 1985, archived on PennSound, in a panel she shared with Rachel Blau DuPlessis at St. Marks Church in New York. It was called "The Tradition of Marginality," in reference to continuing marginalization of women's achievements and opportunities and voices in the Western literary tradition. I was moved and inspired by Kathleen's gumption, intensity, retrospective urgency and honesty. Her vividly embodied nature erupted there, provoking sympathetic argument, thought and action. She seemed angry but was not looking for enemies or fall guys; she accepted herself, I felt, admitted what had happened, what she wanted, what she'd done, in telling how her own personal history in poetry and its social publication matrices had led to her co-founding *HOW(ever)* two years earlier.

I think that project, so sinewy and exploratory, declarative and implicating, queer and direct, must have commanded a lot of anxiety and effort among males back then, myself included, to overcome conditioned, habitual delay and avoidance. This recognition in me as a listener only accentuated the value of the points she was making about the history of women's innovative poetry in a patriarchal culture, including its typical sequestering in seemingly isolated instances and defensively generic and minor alternative classifications.

A straight woman writing experimental, innovative poetry in a city that produced and valued feminist literature insofar as its content drew almost all the attention, preferably radical or lesbian, and given her ambivalence about the social formations and doctrinaire implications marshaling Language Poetry into increasing attention, she'd found it hard to publish or gain credibility, but in the mid-Eighties that was changing. After years of sharing work in intimate regular sessions with co-editors Beverly Dahlen and Frances Jaffer, she'd begun to find common ground with other women and was ready to proclaim noisily and with acute grace her own backstory relative to this project, resonating with women's wider-spread backstory relative to their work's retrospective, remarkably selective canonization up to that time. (Since that time, *HOW(ever)* and other efforts, including Kathleen's, have considerably expanded and deepened recognition of women's diverse, dynamic and astonishing interventions in literature across Western history.)

In the early Nineties, I'd moved to Belmont, MA, for a year and then lived a few years in Stone Ridge, NY, adopting new roles, attachments, functions, and identities. I began to develop a long work with Kathleen in mind, making, I suspect, my own effort to stick out my neck and see what I would say from my unprecedented and still mostly unknown posture. Ergonomically, it was awkward, particularly as I spoke it into a small cassette-tape recorder/player while driving alone an hour each way to and from my job, at which I felt inadequate and naïve to a fault — a major fault — but somehow held my ground.

I called it "ESSAY(S): WHAT I WANT WHY NOT (A DREAM)" and it took the form of a series of paragraphs without evident connections, since they were written at different times and I didn't type them out soon. Somehow this work in process, if not clearly one in any progress, was to my mind dedicated to Kathleen, though I cannot remember specifically why. Maybe I was feeling absent from the Bay Area in ways that caught me up poignantly as reminiscent of her own absences from there, when she was in Rome, when I'd miss her, as well as the rarity of our convening during the half of each year she was in California. Perhaps I imagined through it a link to her, a conduit. And her first book was called *What I Want*, and I still find that compelling.

I can't say who the "you" is in this sample paragraph. Why not Kathleen?

> You wanted something. You chose it. It almost seemed you needed it, and desire was there too. [This written Thursday morning August 17th.] And you got it, an experience that would change your life, or others, or both. In my case, certainly it was partly to find out what the experience was. Not just a curiosity, but a need to know experientially, to know through my body, through development, through awakening, forgetting, and struggle. Then you have to accept all the confusion, regret, inconvenience, agitation, hurt, loss, . . . and risk of destruction implicated in that experience's emergence in a world of material, organic life, and of civilized human compulsion. I don't regret it one bit.[1]

I don't know which year I wrote that, but in late 1995 I decided I'd "revise all the paragraphs by typing them anew (as if into a typewriter) — OK to add thoughts. No fidelity to original required (this a variable value). Essay may be fiction, also. (What's a fiction?) ∴ no need to revise on this page." I appear to have thus executed about ten pages, double-spaced, and to have meant the past nineteen years to get back to it, so I'm glad I made that notation on the original. I no longer can retrieve WordPerfect files frozen on an old computer, so I'll have to retype it all anyway.

I have read those ten pages aloud on a double bill with Carla Harryman at the Ear Inn (in New York), October 1995, having revised them the previous two weeks and somehow also orally improvising other verbiage based on the car tapes that I must have had on headphones along with questionnaire responses from audience members that I tried to integrate or intersperse as I went along.

I tried to recreate/revise that reading in early 2008 when invited to read for the State University of New York at Buffalo, by reading the same ten-page typescript (I still haven't worked more on it nor the other forty pages, though I always want to) while listening on headphones to the 1995 reading of the same material and addressing prompts solicited from the audience by having had slips of paper passed out at various times for them to write down a question and wave the slips over their heads to signal an usher to carry it to me on the stage. (This triumphantly catastrophic event is memorialized in a video tape, also at PennSound.) There, as in its typescript, the project decays into a formless flop that indicates achievement primarily, again, in the form of this writer's neck sticking out far enough in a peculiar enough torque to result in a radically disorganized presence, while still on page/stage.

Kathleen and I exchanged letters in the early Eighties, especially when she asked me to comment on a draft she was preparing for *Ironwood* of a discussion of Language Poetry as she related to it at that time. I wrote four pages single-spaced on my office electric typewriter. My journal then does not reflect my reading of her draft toward my appreciation and criticisms, but it does record my writing there, the same day (it was my 33rd birthday),

> 6/14 Sort of resolutions: I feel like I can + want to
> have experiences of depth + freedom + openness to
> experience + opportunities within the continuity
> of taking care of business. At least I can integrate
> reflection and spiritual values into the will to work
> hard at whatever I do.[2]

From Rome, she responded to my epistle with seven and a half pages, in even smaller font and narrower margins, scribbling in corrections, edits, additional words and phrases for clarity, along with a new draft revision, already sent to *Ironwood* to meet deadline, with more handwritten notations to me in its margins. Work that seemed so effortless and casual on the published page was fiercely, defiantly, painstakingly, urgently developed and layered, questioned and negotiated. (And yes, I responded to hers with another five pages, and she to that with six. Then she returned "home," and we struggled instead with trying to find times to meet up.) Although I gave her quite a hard time about some things in her essay and probably offended her and hurt her more than once in this exchange, she was passionately and appropriately friendly in response.

Other times we sent each other poems to enjoy or critique. I was delighted to know and communicate with her. Kathleen was different, strange, hilarious, emotionally convincing, vehement and analytical in ethics, warm, humane and generous. I closed one letter with the salutation, "friendlily," which charmed her pants off, precipitating her writing in response a poem, "Fried.lily."

She asked me for help in refocusing her attention, as she put it, around this same period, and I loaned her Robert Bresson's short book called *Notes on Cinematography*, written in the Fifties and first published in France in 1975, which she read.

> One does not create by adding, but by taking away. To develop is another matter. (Not to spread out.)

□

> Empty the pond to get the fish.

□

> Against actors' assurance, set the charm of models who do not know what they are.

□

> One same subject changes in accordance with images and sounds. Religious subjects receive their dignity and their elevation from the image and the sounds. Not

(as people believe) the other way about: the images and
sounds receive from the religious subjects...

☐

To an actor, the camera is the eye of the public.

☐

Models. It is to you, not to the public that they give
those things which it, perhaps, would not see (which
you glimpse only). A secret and sacred trust.

☐

An ice-cold commentary can warm, by contrast, tepid
discourses in a film. Phenomenon analogous to that of
hot and cold in a painting.

☐[3]

Despite a translation that I find (in this page chosen *au hasard*) inadequate
to English grammar and construction, I found his text implicitly
delicate and tender while plainly severe and dogmatic, even if framed as
injunctions only for Bresson himself — did he ever want this published?
was he persuaded? — so that it reminded me of Kathleen's personality
and poetry in some ways, while also sapped of metaphor and lyricism, so I
seemed to be offering her an alien transmission. Bresson's intentions were
almost utterly enigmatic in relation to art, life and any sense of Kathleen,
but perhaps in the same ballpark with formalist, Brechtian and Noh
aesthetics. I couldn't really understand why I was so taken with it myself,
but I think it excited my own ambivalence. To press it on her in response
to her request allowed me to sound out an interpretive usage that might
enlighten me.

So I think in retrospect. By the mid Oughts I found myself
perplexedly preoccupied in wondering why she'd written "Bresson

Project: 'Forget you are making a film'"[4] and dedicated it to me, though I knew I'd had something to do with it. She answered with a short letter, lyrical and pointed by turns, spare, modest and loving, as most letters had become, in the new century.

> ...I heard the quote marks and had to begin somewhere. I was looking for a path that would not reveal its swerve except in throwing a stone to the next square ...seeing it land imperfectly, just barely inside the line.
>
> The question shows me that I never entirely comprehended your intention when you stood there to the side of yourself, with your double caught like a bit of shadow in the improvised glare. I wanted that set point. An instruction to push against.
>
> It almost didn't matter what I wrote about...I began in reserve. I was drawing a blank, but the pictures began to appear on the page as if I had suddenly learned to draw film clips.
>
> I said to Bresson, "Steve sent me. Just tell me a position."
>
> He said, "Start drawing."[5]

She attempted an instruction to me, in the form of a strong request, a few years back, to edit David Bromige's work for posthumous collection and publication. Kathleen and I were both close friends of David, and I'd collaborated with him a few times and called or visited him in his last few years of increasing debilitation, physical and mental, before he died of complications in 2009. She protested my refusing this responsibility, which scanned as well beyond my abilities to make time and energy available, despite my love for David and enthusiasm for this project.

I could see devoting myself to it with passion and perspective, but I had no skills or experience in this area and still couldn't assemble a selection of my own, much less any other book to publish, despite lots of products I was proud of, ready for revision or assembly.

If I'd had an academic position, would I have jumped at this project? Listening to Kathleen's experience hadn't encouraged that direction in me. David had always crowed I'd be well off as a psychologist, but a clinician's private-practice income had sunk by half, compared to a generation earlier, by the time I became a professional and a family man; rural Maine paid less than a swank city clientele; time and travel had to be strategically parsed. I disappointed her, our dead David, and myself.

I was always surprised and delighted when Kathleen noticed me and said something about it, as her observations seemed to come from someone to whom my knowledge, my way of knowing, that is, was alien and attractive, a break that proposed an opening. When I told her how I planned to write a poem word by word out loud at the Actualist convention in the South of Market neighborhood (on my older brother's 32nd birthday, 1977), she exclaimed, "Oh, the edge!" provoking me to dedicate the resulting poem, under that name, to her, though she was absent at the performance. I felt she knew me, so, although not much older, she was like a big sister in the mother's place, for me. She could have been my very young mother, delivering me at age fourteen, and very close, though we never have seen one another enough.

> When I think of you, it is at work not at rest. I do not
> know how to explain this leisure without the learned
> habit of apology, yet that would be false. Ambition still
> makes static, but the air is often clear. I write to you
> out of affectionate attachment and severe doubt . . . and
> some memory of another life not quite surrendered. I
> never wanted to make choices. You are able to, each
> time you change body positions or deliver a line. You
> turn on the radio and it's your own voice falling to the

left of you. You are slim and of medium coloring with an often droll expression hovering near your mouth. You are living a life I know nothing of, except through your description and the dream of the black car. Love has always been the motivating force in my life. Someone asks if you've heard from me and you haven't.[6]

This is about her, not about me. But only from my point of view.

November 15th, 2014

1. Steve Benson, manuscript, unpublished, undated, p. 15 (brackets are in the original).

2. Steve Benson, National-brand lined bound notebook, dated 12/9/1981 – 4/24/1983.

3. Robert Bresson, *Notes on Cinematography*, trans. Jonathan Griffin (New York: Urizen Books, 1977), p. 48 (complete).

4. In Kathleen Fraser, *il cuore: the heart — Selected Poems 1970–1995* (Wesleyan University Press, 1997), pp. 74-75.

5. Kathleen Fraser, from a letter to Steve Benson, dated April 1st, 2008, Rome (all ellipses, except the first here, in the original).

6. Excerpted from "Five letters from one window, San Gimignano, May 1981," in Kathleen Fraser, *il cuore: the heart*, pp. 83-84 (ellipsis in the original).

— For Kathleen Fraser

A first encounter, 1985. A lyric mode to touch a tongue that's erstwhile
rendered outside, a slur tumesced with blood pricked from the other side
of the world. There was Blanchot. There was Jabès. Then this — a
distinctly intimate catastrophe of missives, an imperious recusancy
from the propositional trace. This dissembling intransigence pulsed
contra diegesis, that nonetheless reforms the glossalalia of the sentence
as an ordering of fragments, not inceptive but released. *Anything is
interchangeable with a small net. You know that.*

All mother tongues are motherless, and so vest their authority
in subsequence alone; surrender only meaningful if one risks everything,
every possible conformity to structure, or to verge. Living in the aftermath
may lure one to discern the world as system — as assemblage — but the
representation of its attributes makes of that medusa's gaze the feint of
deliquescence, a movement always out of, never into, never towards.
Down the middle keeps tearing. Is torn and wants to.

The reticule can only catch what's larger than its apertures,
a measure always indexed to their frequency in turn. One longs to be
extrinsic, to be aggregated outside. One longs to bring the outside in, a
single chance, an only go — become it. No need to stopper your ears if
the transition is silent. *Untie the boat. Your hands will be woolen. Cover your
ears. We move into stone.*

from *Duration Knows No Law*

φ

The secret labor of instinctual decadence, the faculty of looking around
every corner — this is what it comes to, what my mastery amounts to, as
the minion who has gained the right to sacrifice her sectary by having long-

since sacrificed herself. Have I said it already? There is no other practice; what is possible for others is not possible for me. What is possible for others...the chief thing is to be seen...

φ

Have I said it already? But when I say already I already grow...have already grown distracted. Already distracted, by having been already made to vanish in diathesis, passing from the servitude of passage to the stasis of this standing in the always in between. The present is already... the presence of the present is the ready-made already that, contrived as the submission of what has been to what will be, is given by the suppliance of sense to every passing...every passage...

φ

Weary. And distracted. Wearily distracted is the way of all reprisal. Weary ambuscade portends the triumph of proceeding. Tabetic fumes recoil into substance — into *matter* — where all other formal archetypes adduce such change of state as though the symbol and the symptom of our regress into absence, the portent of our final lurching towards...

φ

All the nothing you see, all the vanishing you phrase — a triumphant prostitution to the future...

φ

To find one's place in history one must linger past its limit, one must step aside. To take the role of doyen one must fill the position — the *position*, I say — of prophetic obsolescence; one must make oneself the bulwark of subjection without conquest, without even the *prospect* of requital, or remise...

φ

These thoughts become too savage to return me to the hope that such opprobrium prefers as an admission, an escape. But perhaps this is enough. But perhaps this is enough. To be regarded. Become at once already once confused. Become distracted. Would like to end. Would like to end. I. A mere moment of clutter initiates our slump into transcendence, if not sacrament. I am learning to have been seen, to have already seen by having been seen. By being seen. Everything else that passes passes over...

φ

Seeing every side precludes the seer from engagement, from the subtle disarray of seeing anything at all. One is first made master of this roiling persistence by surrender to the seignory and camouflage of witness — the *delivery* from praxis — which is equal to an infinite delay...

φ

To imagine oneself virtuous one must first conceive of virtue as a rhapsody of action, regardless of one's subsequent discernment of effects. That there has been forewarning of the difficulties waiting just beyond the next horizon is not reason to avoid it; such pain adduces progress, makes of history the semblance of a reasoned voice. The look back is illumined by the mirror of futurity; no one is a hero to her debtors, or a scoundrel in her zeal for second chances...

φ

Of what's been said already, if not by me then by some other, I neither stand as witness nor believe that such a testament would serve to countermand the dream by which the claim to witness is dissembled, thus confessed. Anyone who might conceive such forfeiture of reasonable affect as a means and not a measure…not a measure to be sure of…To be sure it is no matter to the seity whose prescience understands such vacant canon as a *universal* voice. And this, too — this mattering alone — is of no consequence to one who is as useless in the judgment of her rivals as sequestered in her bishop's cell of longings and intents. Only mattering *together* matters…

φ

The marshalling of one's affiliates into an amalgam of instantaneous reflexes requires the exclusion of everything else. Intolerance is not merely the effect of common orders of kinship — the feint of consanguinity, both compulsive and by choice — but is equally intrinsic to the nature of discernment; to the indolence of being in a world…

φ

There has to be someone — *anyone* — otherwise nothing. The truth of the matter and the mattering alike is made coherent by the idyll of the fragment, the disruption; by the trick of some caesura put upon each ersatz plexus — each perimeter of middles — as a nascent void…

LOVE ACROSS A CROWDED ROOM,
OR,
GIFTS FROM KATHLEEN
——— JEANNE HEUVING

After several years of uncertain and frustrated endeavor as an experimental fiction writer, I turned to poetry. I hadn't been able to discover or construct what I was looking for in fiction, and poetry offered me a more mobile set of relations. As I had with experimental fiction, I began searching literary journals and bookstores for something that I was looking for, but couldn't quite find. I happened upon Kathleen Fraser's then-recently-published *New Shoes* and found a way forward. In starting out with experimental fiction I had been drawn to what Laura Riding calls the "individual unreal," or more loosely what might be called the alienation effect, but my actual life was much taken up with ardent and anxious love and sex. In reading Fraser's *New Shoes*, I discovered a poetic speaker who offered me the open-ended subjectivity of experimental fiction but also an existence I wanted to live. It was lines such as these in *New Shoes* that commanded my unwavering affection and belief:

> I felt myself in love with him watching his tongue run over his lips
> and remembered Fredericka
>   always keeping the tube of vaseline in her purse
> always gliding it over her mouth should there be someone to kiss
>
> and thought how I liked space and long unending lines, how my life
> was that way, without visible connections or obvious explanation

The first time I met Kathleen in person, it was love across a crowded room. We were in the assembled company of women scholars and poets at an MLA roundtable on the woman's long poem and she said something and then I said something (what, I no longer remember) that was working the same groove, and so our eyes met down the long table. It was a few years later that I had dinner with Kathleen, again at a large table of scholars and poets. This time I found a seat directly across from Kathleen and planted myself there. I immediately told her of a dream that kept recurring, of a man stepping into me, as onto a step ladder, again and again. Often he did not succeed, and sometimes he did, and then it was as if our eyes were ringed together. Over and over this man would try to step into me. Haunted by this dream, seduced by it, I hoped it would seduce Kathleen. I was quite sure this dream was about lost love and may have intimated as much — but Kathleen turned the tables. This man was coming into me because he wanted me to strengthen him, she said. He wants your strength, he wants you to make him stronger. I was surprised by this interpretation and in my current state of seeking this dream while awake to be visited by it while asleep, I found myself propelled back into Kathleen's lines in *New Shoes*: "you, on your back, in air, above the couch in the other room, / discover your body below and a girl dreaming of a door." It was the space of the subjunctive, the conjectural, that I had entered into unbeknownst to me, and Kathleen had not stilled this state but prompted me to enter it further: "We are lavish / rooms with many doorways that open out." With Kathleen, it was not to check or stop whatever drew one, but to take it further.

Soon thereafter, Kathleen invited me to be on the editorial advisory board of *How2*, the electronic sequel to her *HOW(ever)*. The invitation came from Kathleen along with a dash of glamour and excitement. I was at another MLA, this time in San Francisco, and Kathleen came and whisked me away for lunch. I was abashed and dazed as we drove through the crowded San Francisco streets. Kathleen was a fast and careful driver and in no time we were seated at a table, words cascading between us. The reason that I had even found myself at these tables of scholars and poets was in good part due to Kathleen herself. Kathleen, through *HOW(ever)*, initiated conversations between women scholars and poets by her insight that the recovery of modernist women's writing was very important for contemporary women's experimental writing and efforts to create community across these groups. This was very important to me because I was both scholar and writer — and the perpetual advice I then received was that I should choose between them, which I could not conceive of doing. Shortly after reading Kathleen's

New Shoes, I had entered into a Ph.D. program, but kept finding some small time for my writing as the demands of the degree program enveloped me.

Soon after our lunch at Zuni, I invited Kathleen for a visit to the Bothell campus of the University of Washington, and she spent a couple of nights in Seattle at my house. We talked a great deal in a stream of uninterrupted conversation. Kathleen listened to me more closely than perhaps anyone ever had and I was surprised by how our conversation rallied. Fresh out of my Ph.D. program, I was much taken up with the then-breaking news of postmodernism and poststructuralism, French feminism and language poetry, so Kathleen's attention to me, and how important it was to me, caught me off guard — a richness of attention that I came to crave. Kathleen offered me a return to my prior writing life before I pursued a Ph.D. because of her unwavering belief in how significant writing comes out of a complex process of the writer's evolving psyche and writerly invention, and because she refused the monumental aspect of the message then — that language was everything — while still listening to this new perspective. I was relieved to hear her pronounce then, and in years following, "that's just cookie-cutter." By this she meant that some kind of model was being followed by someone, as if on rote, or with too much obeisance to foolscap. Hearing her say it then, I felt a great relief, so there is a place for the "me" of "me," something wayward, recalcitrant, not comprehending. Kathleen produced in me, as she had in others, the very possibility of transmogrification, an unmooring.

When I was trying to finish my first creative book, *Incapacity*, and was uncertain of the title, I asked Kathleen if she would mind reading through the manuscript, even if very quickly, to let me know whether she thought the title was right. She told me that the only way she read was with a pencil in hand making emendations as she went. Only then would she know whether the title of the book worked for the book. What came back were several very careful emendations of my text, all in pencil, some tentative, with a question mark attached — a changed article here, a word or two there, a question about the inclusion of certain phrases or segments

— and validation of the title *Incapacity*. I had already passed through a Masters program in creative writing in which I had experienced a great deal of slash and burn by teachers who tried to clean up my poems of their excess words in order to create the publishable item. I had almost always rebelled from these suggestions — but this wasn't what I was trying to do. In contrast, Kathleen was very much inside my book and I experienced the rare gift of an editing that brought the book into itself, myself into myself, more mine, rather than less. And yes, she thought, the title *Incapacity* was a good one. Don't go for the alternative title in the vying, *Offering*, she recommended, because it could be about anything and might convey too much sweetness. Go with something definite, the "the," although the "a" and "an," or no article at all, were also needed, depending.

At this time, I turned with much interest to Kathleen's 1990s publications, *when new time folds up* and *Translating the Unspeakable: Poetry and the Innovative Necessity*. Now the Kathleen of the playful and erotic subjectivity of *New Shoes* was ecstatic. I was thrilled with these lines:

> The letter A is a plow
> (mare pulling into ma*re*)
> > horse plowing sea
> > Maremma
>
> > > Was A
> > > where
> > you made and
> > > unmade your mind . . .

> . . . To have written the sentence's smooth beauty and,
> later, to break it apart . . . . To let the poem pour from the
> closet, long erratic music-tugging lines and word horde
> of the broken-in-on nightlife.

Kathleen's sexual ecstatic operated in tandem with her concern for personhood and its suppression. Her *Translating the Unspeakable* began with this woeful meditation:

> I've always been moved by the double life and bifurcated sensibility of the classical centaur — human torso grafted onto horse flanks and hooves; or Rene Magritte's reverse mermaid, whose sad fish eyes and barely parted lips rest on dry sand, just beyond the waves, mutely grafted to the lower half of the a female body . . . unable to utter even a fragment of wariness. In these creatures it is as if the person-centered part of consciousness must be subdued, subjected and destined to remain without voice . . . untranslatable.

I was unsure in reading this passage whether what was untranslatable was not more valuable than the translation, although Kathleen was quick to mark the cost of a refusal to articulate:

> Learning to move out from under the perception of non-presence, that uncounted / unwritten part of one's experience; entering into the activity of articulation, attempting this struggle within the inhibiting field of established precedent are urgencies...

Through my many interactions with Kathleen, I have been brought more into and out of myself than I would have without her tactful mentorship and lively friendship. Once when visiting Kathleen in San Francisco, I was brought suddenly into myself, reminded of myself. I had gone to San Francisco MOMA to visit a Magritte exhibition Kathleen had already seen. I was much acquainted with Kathleen's "Magritte Series" from having read her *New Shoes* earlier and so pondered especially hard those paintings that were in her series. In the process, I happened on a work that Fraser had not written about, but one that entered into my affective life with a shock of recognition. It was Magritte's late painting "Love Song." In looking at it, I was instantly filled with great sorrow. The entire painting was a monochrome of grays and blues. Two lovers were cemented to a gray concrete block as if barely emerging out of their clayey condition and were mooning together. They were without faces, eyes, and arms, and were glommed onto each other, their rock bodies pitted and their most distinguishing mark rather large belly buttons incised into the rock. They appeared to be male and female because of a slight difference in body size, although they were without genitals. This then was my lost love and me, the girl I had written about in my experimental fiction:

> She herself could fit the bill at the Paradiso Coffee House quite well and felt quite at home there. She managed the look of slight boredom and tiredness that allowed her to fit in. Even amongst the regulars eye contact was kept to a minimum and all but forbidden with those who clearly didn't belong. It was necessary when at the Paradiso to avoid anything akin to self-promotion or a futuristic happiness.

A siren song went through me — and I felt unmoored. From Kathleen, it has been the mooring and unmooring that is so profound — this turning into myself and the great journey of turning out.

When he said "red cloud," she imagined red
but he thought cloud (this dissonance in which she was feeling
trapped, out-of-step, getting from here to there).

— Kathleen Fraser, "Medusa's hair was snakes. Was thought, split inward."

"Write about it," Kathleen said. "Promise me. Write about it tonight."

I had asked her, "What do you make of it, Kathleen, that this is happening in 2014?" After a poetry reading when we were sat chatting like girls in the car outside her home, I had told her about a strange animated moment at Zuni Café, in San Francisco:

First, a little backstory — one afternoon, in the mid-1990s, walking through Zuni with my husband, I passed a well-dressed woman sitting alone at one of the best tables, the light pouring down through the sycamore trees outside onto the tablecloth, etc., as she was reading the *New York Times* and, this is what I envied, extending herself confidently into public space.

As Kathleen and I sat in the car, I mentioned that I had at last, after two decades, tried to realize myself in that same space. I went into the restaurant, in late afternoon, opened a book, and ordered dinner and wine. A woman and her husband came and sat nearby, ordered food, talked about their children. I was eating dessert, when they got up to leave and the woman steered the man ahead of her, awkwardly, but he was moving to the door, and then she stopped and bent toward two women sat at a table opposite me. I heard her say quietly and quickly that she had been watching them and thinking how well they looked, what a good time they were having together alone at the table, and she had liked seeing them there. They smiled. The waitress brought me a second cup of coffee, which I hadn't ordered, and she smiled also.

Can she substitute *dog* for *cloud*, if *red* comes first?
Red tomato.
Red strawberry.
— "Medusa's hair was snakes. Was thought, split inward."

I rose to leave and as I passed the two women one reached out her hand, "Excuse me. Did you have a good dinner? It's great that you come here by yourself. So happy to see you enjoying yourself," she began.

I reminded Kathleen that we had once had lunch at Zuni together, and it had made me laugh that when I gave her name to the hostess, she had said, "Oh, let me show you to Kathleen's favorite table." The table was on the mezzanine, in the gallery looking down to the wood fire and the table where that other elegant woman had sat.

A few years ago, Kathleen was interviewed by Suzanne Stein for a Kelsey Street Press podcast, in which she talked about encouraging her female students at San Francisco State in the 1970s to take up space publicly. She taught a women-only poetry workshop, where, as she described it, "women could learn how to talk."

"Most of my women students were very smart but they could not speak publicly," she says in the interview. It had been the same when she taught at Reed College and also at the Iowa Writers' Workshop, women not claiming their space. " — As I talk about this, I feel my hand going to my throat," she said.

If I were given only one word to describe Kathleen Fraser, it would be "ebullient." Kathleen, my dear, you are a natural dazzler — not in the egomaniacal blowhard sense of so many major writers, who can't rest till they've sucked all the O2 out of the room. No, your ebullience is just that — an actual and very welcoming overflowing, a kind of ecstatic invitation to share in a continual conversation, one constantly renewed by some fresh perception, some vivid sense of surprise. This is not to say that you aren't also a rascally Scottish imp. One never knows what you'll say next. So it is with your poetry. It radiates from a deep concern with the most audacious inquiry. Radical lyric — a sense of experiment as investigation — has always marked your work with its boldly magnanimous spirit.

My first encounter with you, Kathleen, was in 1975, in your poetry workshop at SF State. That didn't work out so well. First there was the fact that I was an utterly lousy poet, more enamored of Keats than O'Hara (whom I'd never even heard of that point). And second. Well, second, your kindness could not recall me from whatever drug-induced redoubt I'd withdrawn to. We did not meet again till some twenty years later, when, as chance would have it, we both found ourselves in Boulder, Colorado, in the backyard of Jane Dalrymple-Hollo and Anselm Hollo, standing in line for Naropa's catered chow. I remembered you instantly, of course — how could one not? From that moment on, a delightful and immensely gratifying friendship was struck up. But it was more than that, of course. Kathleen, you *mentored* me. Not just by graciously giving me pointed advice on my work and then blurbing my first real book, *Burn*, or generously securing an invitation for me to read with Jeanne Heuving at Canessa Park through the good offices of Avery Burns, but in so many other ways, too.

Case in point. About ten years ago I succumbed to the delusion that I was falling in love with a poet of our mutual acquaintance. I was married at the time and so I turned to you, Kathleen, for sage advice — advice, naturally, that was spot on and that I utterly failed to heed. More importantly — in a tradition that has been largely lost, I think — you have, perhaps without even knowing it, counseled me on how to live. I think some of this comes through in our exchange of letters, collected and edited by Jennifer Firestone and Dana Teen Lomax in their wonderful *Letters to Poets: Conversations about Poetics, Politics, and Community*. I wince a bit now whenever I re-read them. My contributions to the conversation are shot through with grad-school wonkiness, while yours overflow with lessons in how to see. Your letters are refulgent with the most enticing details of lived experience — the color of light on a brick wall, or how a painting struck you. I felt humbled by this exchange. It taught me a lot — which frankly I'm still absorbing. But the generosity of your gesture I take to be typical of you: the invitation to enter into a conversation. The dismissal of hierarchy. The sense of acknowledgement in a shared life in poetry and the commitments it entails, the demands it makes, the rewards it gives.

How to adequately express my gratitude to you, Kathleen, for all the largesse you've so casually strewn my way? I've written about your work several times, trying to articulate just what it means to me and its impact on the larger cultural landscape. So I'll close these remarks with an excerpt from my piece "White Blink," written for *Jacket 25* (2004) as a response to your extraordinary poem "WING."

Of course the wing is the figure of an archaic power cutting across a universe founded on — and foundering in — desire. Not the forgetting of the air, but its embodiment. The form by which "the New" lifts itself into itself. The very body of the autopoetic. Which is to say, the poem's evocation of the newly emergent is a swirl of gestures around the notion of presence. A kind of "fall out":

> now and melt with rush all in one place nothing changed   I
> did not grow up I   went away in one phase   brooded I over

> skier   in black the flyer, forces   that dive far yet he
> persists   in contradiction to as does physical pain
> that which is known a way   of crashing in on you   to us
> changing, now perilous

What is it to be present? Neither wholly here, nor wholly not here, comes
the answer. But as an event occupying continually the spaces of its own
liminality, "coming forward in its edges," a hovering and a massing and
a dissolution — the exact motive and stance of *flight*. Which would be
another word for *angelos — angel — messenger — wing*.

> the shimmer of wing, which claim may tell us everything
> in a white blink

Not to be confused with inspiration, that misleading trope for the
intuitions and happenstances of process, but rather "attachment." To
be New is to be both caught up by and advancing the procedures of
attachment. Of joining and belonging. In the space where blankness is
felt, not as the signal of invention's failure, the challenge to utterance, but
as the register and commencement of all that is possible. The telling of the
New is all in the shimmer. The white blink that discloses "everything."
All that we need to know about how to live — it's there, a quicksilver
pulse inside the white shimmer of that wing. And then it disappears.
Consummatus est. If seeing is believing then it is also these larger forms of
flooding and enfolding. The rigorous marshalling of the senses by which
the body trips into the body. A wing is for holding the empty spaciousness
of whatever is said.

This poem asks: can we still say "the angelic" with a straight
face? Here the name of the possible supernal comes forward as a face
full of brilliance, a self-organizing principle in the complex geometry of
chance and revelation, an entire ethics, really:

> It can happen that the intoxicating wing will draw the mind as a
> bow

Tension and release. Dyadic pulse and wingbeat. Uplift of the poem, where "she used words downward." To make the Orphic gesture. Then erase it. Or re-build it. The three Black Quartets of "WING" re-name the poem's engine with the music of a fervent stammering, a violence of the word that alone is equal to the event of the word, to the wing of a language we are just beginning to hear (again). That the poem (the wing) is also a graph: it charts the syllables of its own luminosity, the trace of its passage through a central and abiding darkness that is also the edge of the poem, "not static," but ecstatic. Wing leaping beyond itself. Winging it. Stand *here* and be — outside yourself.

The wing is not some airy construct. To know it we must engage with its "historic tendons." Those ligaments that stretch backwards and forwards in time and across the porous expanse and surface of the body.

> picking, pecking at   our skins ghost or angel
> sent to tell us what   we didn't want to know

The wing articulates a formal structure in time. It carves the air with its purpose. A motion repeating itself. Sustaining the engine of flight one word at a time. A scaffold that hoists the tensions of the word in the very structure of the word. But the wing is a device for telling us that the poem is also made out of intervals, the spaces and pauses between words. *White blink* where everything may happen.

We live inside the erasure, says the wing, of our passage from one place or moment to the next. Inside the tension of repletion and recession. And this is how things get built. The volumes and planes, the spaces for living are erased and lifted, but above all, re-iterated in a continual motion that's both jagged and fluid. This is how the restless energies of the poem construct the door between inside and outside, which is the interstitial space of our real dwelling. The space kept alive through the ongoing reinvention of language. The space of the New, which is the place where we may also hold our dead. The struggle to articulate that place occurs where:

decision and little tasks of pain had tried to lift   a
lucent decision and little tasks of pain had tried to lift   bow

itself the wing not static but frayed, layered, fettered,   furling

This is a poetry that plays along the strands connecting the numinous and the earthly, restoring the fractals of erosion and re-formation into a vibrant expression of the human.

"WING" is a poem that does not so much end, as continue over the horizon. The wing impresses the shape of its ghostly presence like a negative print of itself across the skein of words that have built it. It is a *white blink*. Blank. Absent. Or rather, locatable only in the space between the words. The after-image of its passage — the "vanishing point" where word meets wing and wing is nothing but a furling of the poem. "WING" is all stutter and shimmer, heartbeat and "frayed, layered, fettered, furling." Announcement of the possible. Where history is the re-write of history inside the silent interval that contests the very notion of limit. The wing is bright enough to burn us all.

I first met Kathleen in 2003. I was moving to San Francisco; a friend of mine in Buffalo — where I was coming from — had begun an interview with Kathleen the year before in Rome; it remained unfinished. Linda knew how compelled I was by Kathleen's work; would I mind, she asked, finishing the interview for her. It often occurs to me what a gift that offering was — as was Kathleen's generous openness to the possibility of picking up the thread again with a stranger.

We met in North Beach, at a café at the edge of Washington Square Park that appears not to exist anymore as I try to map it on Google to see if the "street view" option will recall anything more about what unfolded that afternoon. I was in my early twenties, fumbling with many things but in particular, that day, with the pages of notes I had come with. I had read and re-read Kathleen's work, had filled the margins of her books, had arrived with the lengthy, scholarly-sounding questions I thought I was expected to arrive with. If I didn't register the foolishness of it then, as I reread that interview now, I do: the stuffiness of my inquiries that Kathleen, each time, so tactfully opened up and let breathe, as she responded with stories of what had spurred each of her projects into being, as she turned the questions I posed around and asked them back at me, as she answered thoughtfully and not under the weight of any particular discourse, deliberately, precisely *because* it was her own.

We talked for nearly two hours before Kathleen observed that it was a beautiful day and we ought to continue across the street in the park. We sat cross-legged in the sun, the recorder between us. We shifted. We lounged. We talked on. I forgot about my notes, the marginalia; I dropped the formality. Kathleen's way of being present didn't leave much room for it. We must have gone elsewhere that afternoon, after the park, because at some point in those recordings the tape stops and picks back up again with an entirely new assortment of background noises. When I returned home late that day, I had nearly six hours of voice to work with. This is a long way of telling a few simple things: the spaciousness Kathleen created and held, the ease of being-with, her generosity with her time, not only the inquiry but also the inquiry *around* inquiry. "You are trying too hard

/ to enter this world. The door is open." This was one takeaway from that first encounter. Another had to do — or are they not different things? — with the kind of presence I will want to have with younger generations of writers, if ever I have the opportunity to be that presence.

Kathleen said something about correspondence that day that strikes me again as I look back on that interview. I had asked her about the letter — a genre, a mode, she often turns to in her poems. I had said something about its communicative one-sidedness. She responded:

> Interesting that you think of letters as one-sided, in
> the sense of there not being an answering response
> from the receiver, a dialogue. Early on, letters were a
> natural place for me to begin from a state of isolation
> or disconnection, simply to get the writing started,
> by addressing an/other when I wanted to write and
> couldn't. I addressed friends with whom I had an on-
> going mental conversation, whose presence pulled
> material and observation from me that I might not get
> to on my own. When I wrote the sequence "Five letters
> from one window, San Gimignano, May 1981"... I'd
> consciously set a problem for myself: to sit at the same
> place in front of a window as the light changed between
> 4 and 7:39pm, writing as many letters as I could in that
> time. I wanted to see what would arrive in this space
> and to use the notes as starting points for gathering
> materials called forth by the particular nature of each
> friend I addressed — in this way framing from different
> physical and speculative angles the new place in which
> I found myself. In that sense, the other person was very
> much there — in my mind — as the 'evoking spirit.'

I suppose it could have occurred to me that afternoon that an interview could be as "one-sided" as I was sure a letter was; yet Kathleen didn't let it be. She asked as many questions of me that day as I asked of her. She listened as intently as if she was the one recording. What followed this interview were years of correspondence between the two of us; and I found what she had said about the letter to be ever more true: that yes, "correspondence" was very much part of the work — *her* work — of being a writer, a way of positioning and re-positioning at varying sites of address. I think her poems — even the ones that don't call attention to themselves as letters — by virtue of the voices they sometimes take up, the imagined bodies they sometimes inhabit, suggest the degree to which this mode has both organized and dis-organized (I mean this as in, the organs of the body, the organs of sense) her poems. But also that it was a way of touching down with deep attention to that "particular nature" of each new encounter, with a deep interest in those connections as they form not only in and through, but also beneath and beyond, "this / language we come up against." "Ah, the sound of one brain flapping," she began one e-mail; "what a royal relief." "I had thought to call earlier… but sort of stubbed my toe — or was it *your* toe — on the non-existent door jamb." I received stories about arrivals and departures, encounters, moments of recognition, responses to books she was reading, *this* about a phone bill: "My heart is light. I may even be able to face balancing a broom on my chin — or my checkbook, on my left foot, being only in arrears, 2 & ½ months (true confessions)." And in the midst of this marvelously persistent play was always something about how she'd thought of me when such-and-such an event occurred; or that it had struck her that I would enjoy this-or-that show she had just seen; or she just met so-and-so whom I *must* meet as well, we'd have so much to share with each other, could she please put us in touch?

Kathleen. As attentive to her addressee as she was to the language of address. And vice-versa. It is a very rare thing to be able to hold both attentions at the same time.

When I open *il cuore* and *Translating the Unspeakable* to write this — which maybe, after all, *is* a dialogue with Kathleen — papers fall out of both. I find notes to friends and near-strangers I have loaned these books to; I recognize in them Kathleen's invitation to dialogue in letter form. I mean I realize these invitations that I've extended to others are stuck in the pages of a collection of selected poems written in, and as, conversation with other poets, other artists, other poems, other works of art. I think of the ways these reachings have made me a part of this ongoing invitation. I turn to one of the pages in *il cuore* that has perhaps been dog-eared since 2003; it is, of course, "Five letters from one window." At 7:39, Kathleen writes to Andrea:

> I'm trying to find a way to include these states of
> uncertainty… the shifting reality we've often talked
> about — fragments of perception that rise to the
> surface, almost inadvertently, and come blurting out
> when one has lived in intense desire and frustration…
> why deny this partialness as part of our writing? Why
> not find formal ways to visually articulate its complexity
> — the ongoing secret life — without necessarily making
> it a candidate for the simple-minded "confessional?"
> Writing is, in part, a record of our struggle to
> be human, as well as our delight in reimagining/
> reconstructing the formal designs and boundaries of
> what we've been given.

I read this on the same afternoon I read many other words of Kathleen's — written over decades — that register humanness, our fallibility, our imperfections, inadequacies, messiness, incompleteness. "Suppose we are a fragment." "[A]s though we were designed to bring forward two opposing sets of facts and bathe ourselves in the resulting struggle." "I suggest solutions and / am full of holes." I don't think Kathleen's work suggests that there is anything inherently in our being-human that can redeem us of our humanness. I think it offers, instead, curiosity, honesty, attention, the very articulation of everything that we are and wish we were and wish we weren't (although dammit, we *aren't* those things and we *are* those others), as modes of redemption that are at the same time only-ever-partial and utterly-complete. "Holes," after all, are the sites at which "something gives in / to a pulse." Misunderstanding opens out onto "other lives." The uncertainty of perception is an entryway to possibility: "the hand on a doorknob that could be / possibly / turning." "Lines / could be sides. There could still be / snow." "The accidents," Kathleen claims, "interest me." And so here we are in the grass, learning not to try so hard to enter the world we are already in. Perhaps because all that trying means we don't see we are already there, or that we refuse that this could *be* that world, because *this* world is imperfect. Kathleen's work asks us to sit, simply, in "the absolute quiet of something about to arrive." To be there with a tape recorder but to let go of the notes we came prepared with. To trust the generosity of what we come face-to-face with, even if that doesn't end up being entirely the case — and it often doesn't. And to recognize that it might take somewhere between all afternoon and a lifetime to be present for the something that does, in fact, show up.

Kathleen Fraser is one of my life's companions. Along with her other gifts, we should add a genius for friendship. I first caught sight of her on the San Francisco State University campus. In 1972 she was invited to be the Director of The Poetry Center. I was a grad student, ambitious and shy, and I viewed that position as only slightly less important than the Presidency of the United States. And there she was, eating an apple as she walked between classes. I would have liked to talk to her, but I was too shy.

I don't remember our first meeting, but Kathleen does. In that era, the two main venues for poetry in San Francisco were The Poetry Center and Intersection for the Arts in North Beach. Kathleen attended a reading there and I happened to be on the bill and, she says, she liked my work. The first exchange I remember is when both our cars were being repaired at a gas station on the south side of 24th St between Church and Sanchez (it no longer exists). We had a long talk standing on the sidewalk. It turned out we both lived in the neighborhood. There I was, chatting with Kathleen Fraser as though that was perfectly normal. Being taken seriously is a serious thing when you are twenty-five, unpublished, from Cleveland Heights and the outer darkness of LA. I became an intimate of her household on Jersey St. She's singing in the kitchen while cooking dinner — she has a beautiful voice — or we drink wine and listen to jazz, hanging out on her red Victorian loveseat, reading each other's work, making suggestions, reporting on our romantic lives, dissecting the latest poetry-world hubbub. These were hours of perfect friendship. Once we talked about old souls and young souls — it seemed to me that Kathleen was a young soul because her life was a fresh adventure. She met people and experiences with fresh surprise and she still does. By 1978 we were both single, and we often went to parties and events together — she had a glimmering black dress I liked, I called it her star-spangled night.

Here is an excerpt from "Wordsworth," a poem of mine from that time:

> Seven hours earlier Kathleen lifted a heavy sizzling
> lid. The chicken, orangy & pink & hopelessly tender,
> nestled in a nest of carrots & leeks. I said, "It looks like

more than itself." I was filled with the sweetness of civilized pleasure and with feeling of reconciliation to a borrowed European childhood that began as a nativity scene under a tree.

And here is an excerpt from an essay called "Allegory," published in *Ironwood* (1984). I discuss a poem that I first read on Kathleen's Victorian settee.

Kathleen Fraser's poem "Medusa's hair was snakes. Was thought, split inward" begins, like most allegories, in a state of perplexity.

> I do not wish to report of Medusa directly, this variation of her writhing. After she gave that voice a shape, it was the trajectory itself in which she found her words floundering and pulling apart.

The first line slyly alludes to eyes averted from the fatal Medusa and, more importantly, tells us indirection will be the theme. The "variation"? — words and communication generally. Having been given a shape, language is "writhing." Fraser brings the myth to a local problem, local event.

> When he said "red cloud," she imagined *red* but he thought *cloud* (this dissonance in which she was feeling trapped, out-of-step, getting from here to there).

Language is gender-identified and the conflict is staged within the sign. Put another way, postmodernism loves-hates modernism's revolt from representation. It isn't only the sublime/undifferentiated in "Medusa" that's being grasped, but an attempt — via detours and hesitations — to recover a true local with its interruption and plurality: what *can* be known, which may be problematical, even just a set of relationships. As opposed to the confines of a false local:

> Historical continuity
> accounts for knowing what dead words point to
> [...]
> M. wanted her own.
> Kept saying *red dog. Cloud.*

Medusa needs the possibility of interpretation, doubling, "thought split." Red can pun for *read* dog, *read* cloud. *Red*: the emotional adjective set against the factual nouns — "she *imagined*... he *thought*." Fraser's poem works at once as a story and example, the poem itself a site of multiple readings, of the "voices" (current poetry usage for allegory, it seems to me) that influence, surround, inform and are our lives.

> Can she substitute *dog* for *cloud,* if *red* comes first?
> Red tomato.
> Red strawberry.
> As if all this happens on the ocean one afternoon in July,
> red sunset soaking into white canvas. The natural world.
> And the darkness does eventually come down.
> He closes her eye in the palm of his hand.
> The sword comes down.
> Now her face rides above his sails, her hair her splitting tongues.

The "distance" between signifier and signified that characterizes much experimental writing is given a local meaning. And there are other dimensions in allegorical writing. Space is patterned (the sunset is a painting of a sunset) and time (the story as metaphor). The glimmer of the distance between commodity and non-commodity is a dimension too, and desire with its own time and space, and death. Red is a sound or verbal token; a cloud or sunset or blood; subjectivity; allegory.

This writing joins a modernist tradition that sees itself as besieged by or besieging linearity — for feminists, patriarchal linearity. The new elements are the sublime and the local: they establish ties to readers' actual lives both in keeping with the tenets of the women's movement and in the spirit of a postmodernism that wants writing to know its readers. Fraser's Medusa is a sublime multiplicity, a myth apprehended through language, through cultural mediations like the Renaissance iconography of "now her face rides above his sails." Medusa is born of an actual conflict — she does not want her language to "point," she wants the voluptuousness and risk of all meanings at once. So the poem is an allegory about allegory.

Kathleen was the first person from the big world to take my writing seriously, as she took my suggestions about her poems seriously. My story is duplicated in the lives of many other writers. Kathleen gave us the gift of her attention and she helped us find our direction without following any agenda. She wants the voluptuousness and risk of all meanings at once.

THE NEW MOON'S ARMS (FOR KATHLEEN)

LATASHA N. NEVADA DIGGS

an angel stands in technicolor as cosmonauts look out

— "COLOR: VIA DELLA PENITENZA"

madam moth's trickster jaromi is dazzling in its
unmasked mystique. green papaya & frothy Thai ice tea. feathers
along w/ dis golden grain. mantra giggle gift & precious cut
away stacking letters so that the celestial meanders. tango as
madame would in Rome. mark the characters cantata. as such

    in emails, she refers to me as
    Ornette Coleman's side-kick with Ella's genes

to abide by tempo in her glance, we suit up for galaxy jumps. if
woman's declaration were rudely bombastic, she'd say necessary. from
poems, we perch & glean between transparency. pounded tissue
outlines dis architecture she bakes. her story of Loisaida or
how she radiated w/ Jazz for modern women somehow stiffened
proudly from a curved note. *purr*. I blush through dis taffeta cheesecloth

she loves my accordion cheese. free the reeds. open
w/ avowal dis honest heart. tether through,
transpose on paper mâché. grow whimsical in words a
Mars trait. I've misread emails. not slowly enough. shaft tunnels. shaft
beams. Issac Hayes. as she implies, directions become baroque. I
missed my flight. I puppet through dis embarrassment. I am
now at the market where everyone loves her Obama badge. not
like we two are "brain dead." we embrace tempers. we rams of
a particular chart. in Venice, I ponder nero di sepia her taste, that
we fancy to play hookey. dis, another swankolious feather

    —*whissper*

hers is a smile that washes "gold from streams" called upon warm
cider pucker. commission *Astor Piazzolla* to croon. vivid light
bellows. *pillow-slumber*: may we roller skate? I pluck deep from
dis cavity my wee gift: a novel set in a mythical Carib. a tinkle toward orange
walls framed beside merfolk. in her: Marjorie. ping-pong master &
winged scholar of turmeric redwood & gangly yellow
she might murmur "soul work." she invites spaghetti. we BART regions
beside Hathor's distortion. even during meteor showers, Mesha never falls

1. The poem, a refurbished golden shovel, contains three lines from the following poems:
COLOR: VIA DELLA PENITENZA, THE UNDERDRAWINGS, WING: VIA
VANVITELLI, written by Kathleen Fraser. These appear in the collection *WING*.
The poem also includes fragments of email correspondences between Fraser and myself
between 2007 and 2008. Jaromi is the word for a front gap that is considered beautiful
in the kikuyu culture in Kenya. Mesha is Sanskrit for Aries.

FOUR LETTERS FROM ONE WINDOW

BRIAN TEARE

Dear Kathleen—

A warm day after a month and more below freezing. The snow's almost melted, the last of it in piles in the parking lot. Veil and revelation, February has a newly frangible texture where it's pocked with thaw. Ice does this lace thing at its edges black as a handkerchief dragged through oil and ash, a fabric that, when unwrapped, discloses neighborhood trash: Styrofoam peanuts, plastic bottlecaps, cigarette butts.

This winter I've been thinking about *WING*, the book and your poem. The book's cover's the visual texture and color of ice just beginning to give way to rain, a whiteness physically intact but dimpled and roughened gray. Seduced by the ways the text is touched by its setting, I can't separate the poem from its context as a book, the way its title page at first seems adhered to the sheer Japanese end papers. As I lift it, it's as though the Unryu peels away from the type, leaving the title — *W I N G* — behind like a transfer. Now I can see the text paper's smoother texture nonetheless echoes the cover's, both handmade in Montreal. I hold in my hands a snowdrift that's been sliced into sheets, their edges deckled where they trickle onto sidewalk.

Of course my inability to separate *WING* from its book has everything to do with *ekphrasis*. By which I mean the book Dale made to hold your poem is itself a reading of it, an interpretative frame I miss when I encounter the text elsewhere. "as if memory were a thick creamy paper," you write in the poem's first of ten sections, words that Dale pressed into thick paper more ice than cream, words I always remember printed thus. And when I read, "its feathers cut as if from tissue or stiffened cheesecloth," the words reinforce *WING*'s hewn materiality, the way Dale designated the top of each page to be the straight edge fed into the Vandercook's grippers, whereas the fore and bottom edges are deckled, the book as a whole a collation of elegant irregular feathered textures indeed ranging from tissue to stiffened cheesecloth.

The book open in my hands, this is what I think about: how the ekphrastic project registers everywhere its response to another text. All the parts of Dale's book articulate themselves *around* your poem, like a mouth as it speaks a word, the made physical shape inextricable from the word that issues from it. And yet your poem "WING" is itself an ekphrastic project, one that draws upon works by Mel Bochner and Jess. I'd argue that there isn't a level of it — page, stanza, line, word, syllable, letter, the spaces around them — that doesn't speak of this relation. Why, if Dale's reading of "WING" references neither Bochner nor Jess, and so they remain hidden by the book as an object, does the book feel so complete? Does such hiddenness allow, as you suggest, "The New [to come] forward in its edges in order to be itself"?

Yours,
Brian

WING

KATHLEEN FRASER

Dear Kathleen—

Why write letters? Many of my favorites among your poems include them. "Dear Narcissus," you've written, "Dear Bob," "Dear Annalisa," "Dear Michael," "Dear Susan." There is in your work, alongside abstraction, the immersion in relationship, process, and the quotidian that a letter exemplifies. And though "WING" includes no letters, I've been thinking of its *ekphrasis* as an epistolary form that addresses the artist indirectly, one in which abstraction carries the weight of relationship. "Dear Mel," "WING" seems to say, "Dear Jess."

For years I glossed over the notes at the end of "WING." Re-reading them recently, I was surprised to find I'd forgotten that the poem is *for* Bochner, and that it was written in direct response to work shown in New York and Rome; you also write that Jess's "wing delivered my point of focus for entering and retrieving certain materials of this poem." I love that you name two modes of relating to another artist's work: a physical encounter that evokes response, a psychic entry into the process of art-making itself. Your poem taught me — and now serves as a reminder of — one of abstraction's great compositional virtues: it makes the physical encounter and the psychic entry equally figural, gestures whose origins become indistinguishable by design.

It wasn't until this winter that I got curious about Bochner. I tracked down the slim exhibition catalogue from his 1988 show at the David Nolan Gallery. Looking for the first time at his drawings — most of them charcoal on paper — I began to realize how crucially a record of your encounter with his work "WING" is. The most immediate revelation: that my favorite poems in the series, the quartets, derive their form from how Bochner would lay four separate sheets of rectangular paper in adjacent relation so that a "blank" square centers the drawings whose repeated cubes are emphatically skewed out of true. Your quartets generally treat each stanza like a discrete sheet of paper, and this treatment mimics some of the effects Bochner's drawings achieve;

the visual elegance and beauty of "Second Black Quartet," for instance, sit in uneasy relation to its syntactical choppiness, so that design takes precedence over semantic meaning. Crucially, however, though design displaces semantics at the center of meaning, it quite deliberately places a new center — a blank square — where semantics once was.

Upstairs, my neighbor sings late into the night. She practices scales, intervals, slowly, a pleasant mezzo. I gain as much comfort from her discipline and diligence, though I couldn't say why, as I do from her music's regular presence. If it is to succeed as a fiction, epistolary form shouldn't repeat information the receiver of the letter already knows. In regards to your own poem, my letters to you might fail, but I hope they will be successful in another way. In imitation of the music through which I came to know your work, I want to tell you what I've learned from it, how it continues to teach me. I like how architecture darkens the voice that visits me through the ceiling.

As ever,
Brian

7 - First Black Quartet, 1988

VIII. SECOND BLACK QUARTET

as does that
which is of
crashing to
us changing
their spots   aware your own she
heart stop   she used words like
downward who   brilliance turning
but are you   he had in my hand

swimming through   struggling
color, I was burn   dictum and
hot gills' events   plain as
cold hand touched   a particular
                     attraction
                     treads some
                     thing cleft
                     if marked

Dear Kathleen—

An endlessly distracted day: errands led to emails led to errands led
to a mind ill at ease. Once home, the window became an extravagance
I couldn't afford. I turned my back on it, but street sounds followed:
garbage can, gate slam, bus brakes, a waitress talking on her cell as she
took a smoke break. Losing focus, I turned back to "WING"'s first
section, "THE UNDERDRAWINGS," where I read "as if each dream
or occasion of pain had tried to lift itself/entirely away, contributing
to other corners, planes and/accumulated depth." Within the lines I
discerned an analogy: what lies beneath a drawing or painting — paper,
gesso, underdrawing — supports it the way dreams or pain may lie
beneath and support abstract form.

 For a long time I was so absorbed by the poem's visuality and
abstraction, I couldn't see that histories of pain form the underdrawings of
"WING": on the one hand, Mel Bochner's *Via Tasso* and the Holocaust;
on the other, Joe Brainard's death and the AIDS crisis. Now I see how,
through the poem's ekphrastic relation to Bochner's 1993 installation at
a former Nazi prison in Rome and the poem's dedication to Brainard's
memory, historical traumas form a crucial part of the poem's support
without over-determining its surface. "WING" is indeed "attached to its
historic tendons... grieving, stressed." Such history, you write in "First
Black Quartet: Via Tasso," "persists as does pain // have a way of crash
// ing in on you, swimming // through matter heart // rate in each cell." I
think cell / room / stanza; I think blood / cell / virus. The word *cell* strikes
like a match against the poem's surface where it flares, illuminating the
abstract with the light it casts.

 By the light of the word *cell*, I see the four stanzas of the "First
Black Quartet" as rooms on the Via Tasso where Nazis held prisoners
during their occupation of Rome, rooms where Bochner later laid down
three army blankets and then on top of each of them arranged burnt
matchsticks into six-pointed stars. By the light of the word *cell* I see

stanzas translate into rooms that turn into cubes, the ones so prevalent in Bochner's 1988 show, charcoal lending their edges a soft smeary aura. By the light of the word *cell* I see the *char* in charcoal and the tip of each matchstick. "A cube's clean volume," you write," shatters and reassembles // its daily burnt mark // the New is used and goes // backwards into match // sticks."

By the light of the word *cell* I also see how Brainard and his partner Kenward Elsmlie enter the poem, and with them a different precarity of embodiment. In section 1, "there are two men, they are tall men, and they are talking softly / among the disintegrating cubes." Later, in section 9, "There are two men without feet, they are tall men swimming through matter." I've always been haunted by those "disintegrating cubes," and though I now have Bochner's cubes as literal antecedents, the disappearance of the men's feet still persists as a kind of parallel disintegration, one that might subtly speak to the gay body politic of the time. Today my ear has caught on the phrase "swimming through matter," noting how it has itself swum through the poem, from section 2 to sections 7, 8 and 9. Today the poem seems to navigate through history utilizing the recursion of Bochner's serial works: phrasing and imagery repeat until their materiality comes to stand for event, "as if each dream or occasion of pain had tried to lift itself / entirely away, contributing to other corners, planes and / accumulated depth."

It's almost midnight in Philadelphia, the street noises minimal, a low hum of rubber. I turn back to the window and see for the first time how it is made of black cubes.

Goodnight,
Brian

(Floating letter, unnumbered, undated)

Dear Kathleen—

It is another late winter, another February. Even the sidewalks look cold. I mean it's below freezing and without snow, and the water in the concrete seems to have risen to the surface as a slight rime of frost. I like how this looks, each sidewalk panel an irregular variegated white sheen over light gray. But really I am writing to you about beauty. And pleasure. I mean the beauty of the book and the beauty of the poem are unembarrassed, as is the pleasure I take in them. "Its / likeness," you write of the wing antecedent to the poem, "consists of strength, atonality, pigment, emptiness and / shafts partly hollow." Is this how "WING" defines its relationship to beauty?

Strength: "a cube's clean volume   shatters and reassembles."

Atonality: "as does that
            which is of
            crashing to
            us changing
            their spots
            heart stop
            downward who
            but are you."

Pigment: "swimming through
            color, I was burn   struggling."

Emptiness: "lucent   marked."

Shafts partly hollow: "We see the delicate marks along the
                    feather and we follow, now to define or depict
                        the outskirts of
                        meaning."

Such definitions of beauty do not preclude "the ghost or angel/sent to tell us
what/we didn't want to know." Inclusive of literal and figurative distress,
error, misprision and misalignment, all the residues of historical trauma,
the poem finds in design a visual equilibrium, wresting from collage and
syntactical violence a form of poise. It's poise with obvious torque, and
though its surface effects are beautiful, duress has lent it a texture that
attests to how "the cube arrives on a day called 'the darkest day.'" And yet,
miraculously, it's a poem, like the months after winter solstice, whose
duration progressively fills with light: these late pages, "these retinal bodies
larger, remarkable for their iridescence."

                    Thank you,
                        Brian

Dear Kathleen—

In anticipation of this final letter, I've been re-reading Norma's *Mars*, the book with Jess' paste-up on the cover. The wing, your "point of focus for entering and retrieving certain materials of the poem," arcs its stony span upward. But so do these lines of Norma's, the title poem's opening: "Now / makes the sequence didn't know and couldn't know. // set within / rough wing / spread hand." Her lines make me want to admit how much there remains to be thought and said about your poem, both because knowledge escapes me and because it simply escapes.

But what if questions were a kind of knowledge? What if experimental prosody weren't an extension of the poet's body (á la projective verse) but an extension of the designer's eye? What if the lyric were the end result of a syntactical process of accretion and stripping away, an abrading of semantics' surfaces? What if the lyric turns out to be one of the plastic arts after all? Like process or knowledge, such questions doesn't vanish without evidence: "in partial erasure," you write, "even bits of pearly rubber, matchstick and lucent plastic / leaving traces of decision and little tasks performed." Consider these letters also to be "traces of… little tasks performed."

And doesn't the poem also, as it progresses, begin to leave "traces of decision," to recycle more and more of its language, using previous sections (and the underdrawings in particular) as source materials and support, shredding them into phrases with great violence until this process becomes the poem's form. Sections 7 through 10 foreground this way of working, though sections 8 and 10, the second and third "Black Quartets," demonstrate this most clearly. Though at first I loved the visual daring and elegance of these pages, now I am most moved by the way the visual does violence to semantic meaning and more representational modes of ekphrasis, especially how the "Third Black Quartet" admits to the "necessity" of the "partial erase" in order for "the

New" to come forward. And yet these erasures are themselves "little tasks of pain": dear Mel, dear Jess, dear Joe.

The brief thaw vanished yesterday, and this morning it's snowing. Just when I'd gotten used to looking at the usual black top of the parking lot, it's white again — asphalt showing only where pedestrians cross it, pulling up snow with their tread, though their footsteps fill back in quickly. Coming as I do from the South by way of the West, I'm still excited by these hours of snowfall. Visually, snow has an abstract life, distilling everything down to geometric gestures it then amplifies with whiteness. And then there's its silence, how it draws sound into itself so that the essential elements of the visual come forward into relation ever more clearly. It's hard not to feel enchanted by the city's transformation: figure and ground vanish into a plane of shapes.

Watching the snow at work, I realize this is what Dale's reading of *WING* in part allows to happen: the ekphrastic ground of the poem recedes not once but twice: first beneath the abstraction of the poem, and next beneath the materials of the book. Though an informed reading of the poem can reveal again both figure and ground relations and points of focus and entry, I sometimes wonder if this kind of reading doesn't in some way run counter to the spirit of the poem and its life as a book object. And then I open the poem to section 5, which begins, "Even the New is attached or marked by attachment // the shimmer of wing, which claim may tell us everything / in a white blink." One of the things I've always admired about your work is that it isn't a puritanically abstract practice — it owns its attachments and the marks they leave.

With love,
Brian

forward edge itself to be volume by necessity as if partial   erase
edge itself to be volume by necessity as if partial erase   other
itself to be volume by necessity as if partial erase   corners
to be volume by necessity as if partial erase   planes
be volume by necessity as if partial erase   accumulate
volume by necessity as if partial erase   depth
by necessity as if partial erase   condensed
necessity as if partial erase   in
as if partial erase   preparation
if partial erase   stagework
partial erase   historic
erase   tendons
of   elaborate
pearly   ribcage
lucent   marked
decision   midway
and   with
little   grains
tasks   of
of   light
pain   talking
had   softly
tried   among
to   distintegrating
lift   cubes
to lift   the
tried to lift   falling
had tried to lift   wing
pain had tried to lift   will
of pain had tried to lift   draw
tasks of pain had tried to lift   the
little tasks of pain had tried to lift   mind
and little tasks of pain had tried to lift   as
decision and little tasks of pain had tried to lift   a
lucent decision and little tasks of pain had tried to lift   bow

itself the wing not static but frayed, layered, fettered, furling

Philadelphia, February 2014

In Kathleen Fraser's work, the new is always arriving, a fidelity to art, the practice & theory & living example.

"…an inclination towards sound/ drifting through the cities…" (31)
In her scenes, in her stanzas, sometimes the woman is looking indirectly, at angles, through gradations of color, through incidents. Or silence.

"this. notes. new year." (39)

As she looks to and through the poem of the world, discovering & inventing patterns, she finds what does not betray her experience…
SHE HAS WORKED INSIDE THE CURVES THAT ARE STRAIGHT, OUTSIDE A SENTENCE THAT STOPS AND STARTS, OUTSIDE AN EXPLANATION…

"These experiments may be modified to infinity…" (89)

She looks for what will live on its own. The poem is precarious but certain. Included in features of her senses: the unacknowledged work of women, many landscapes, household arts, masterpieces by many, the heart.

"The great system of perfect color…" (132)

She thinks of formal arrangements as a spiritual quest: she does not allow materials or edges to stop her. The words for color are the color. They are colors in between colors—mauve—

The women accompany her work. She accompanies theirs, even those she does not know. "The widows of whiter than butter…" (137)

Peter Quatermain notes in his introduction to *il chore: the heart* that some of Fraser's companions are Wallace Stevens, George Oppen, and Barbara Guest.

She helps change the image and expands it—not in the name of a cause—

"It can happen that the intoxicating wing will draw the mind as a/bow" (186)

The living features of her writing include intervals, brushstrokes, red, her struggle, a shepherd's mauve socks. Space was always an active feature of her writing. In the 80s, it continues around the margins of the page, in shadow, expanding a vocabulary of visual art, an homage to all forms of line.

From Stevens she channels the commitment to the aesthetic quest as an important way of being human. A mind playing over activities of art.

Fraser recognizes the struggle of the artist is central…as the mind's situation meets the landscape in the very core/cuore of the activity…

" 'Be a flame for them to pass through,' you advised me," she quotes her artist friend.

From Oppen, she retrieves the commitment to the physicality of language, to the object of the word. She keeps her commitment to perception.

"The letter A is a plow (mare pulling into mare)" (106)

From Guest, she retrieves a commitment to process, to ceaseless experiment. The processes of the writing branch on the page.

She passes these things along: in the art: in publishing: in teaching. From traditions alternative to the narrative and anecdotal yet including them, she encourages women writers to bring a sense of personal exploration, personal form.

She is an inspiration to artists—to her friends, her students, women writing outside the tradition of other...

HOW(ever) is full of experiments, notes, process writings. Its freshness, its creamy pages, folded over...

It arrives in the mailbox, when in the 80s in the Bay Area you might look to see what poetry is. *HOW(ever)* offers freedom, a different codex, a venue.

ɔt ̽ ╱t ̽ ···· ◡ ╱── ╲ ⌒ ∘ ⌒⌒── ╱ ╱⌒ ♮ ··· ◡◡t‴ ◡◡

TO HELP FIND & FORGE A WOMEN'S EXPERIMENTAL TRADITION NOT EXCLUSIVE TO WOMEN...

That can include mothers, unknown women. It can include lesser known men falling down and getting up again. She includes Jack Spicer.

Lines at the edge of the page fall over, risking their bodies to the lack of recognition, knowing mostly the work will mostly not be recognized by the official venues but going on with the break-through work...

Fraser notes, the life is your own form. It can be procedural but it doesn't have to be tidy. The writing can exist at the edges. Lines can be feathery, flame-like and free.

OVER THE DECADES, SHE LOOKS THROUGH ARCHITECTURES—EXPLORING AND EXPLODING THE SONNET FORM (NEW TIME FOLDS UP) AS WALLS ARE EXPLODED IN HER HOUSE—

She folds in many arts. Renaissance arts, Modernist poetry, Etruscan letters, Bill Evans, the fragmentary & the full. The between

is a place for her. A practice.

To make a story with time, she finds an infinite tale. It is likely there is no destination but a continuous living context.

(Quoted lines are from Kathleen Frasers' *il cuore: the heart: Selected Poems 1970–1995*)

POETRY BOOKS

Change of Address. San Francisco: Kayak Books, 1966

In Defiance of the Rains [with Judy Starbuck, prints]. Santa Cruz, CA:
Kayak Books, 1969

Little Notes to You from Lucas Street. Urbana, IL: The Penumbra Press,
1972

What I Want. New York: Harper & Row, 1974

Magritte Series. Berkeley, CA: Tuumba Press, 1977

New Shoes. New York: Harper & Row, 1978

Each Next, narratives. Berkeley, CA: The Figures, 1980

Something (even human voices) in the foreground, a lake. Berkeley, CA:
Kelsey Street Press, 1984

Notes Preceding Trust. San Francisco: The Lapis Press, 1987

Giotto, Arena. Elmwood: Abacus, 1991

when new time folds up. Minneapolis: CHAX Press, 1993

il cuore: the heart — Selected Poems 1970-1995. Hanover, NH: Wesleyan
University Press, 1997

Discrete Categories Forced into Coupling. Berkeley, ca: Apogee Press, 2004

m o v a b l e TYYPE. Callicoon, NY: Nightboat Books, 2011

ARTISTS' BOOKS (limited editions)

b o u n d a y r [with Sam Francis, acquatints]. San Francisco: The Lapis
Press, 1988

from a text [with Mary Ann Hayden, oil encaustics]. 1992

WING [with David Marshall, drawings]. Mill Valley, CA: Em Press,
1995

h i dde violeth i dde violet [collaged from original Fraser poem].
Vancouver: Nomados, 2003

WITNESS [with Nancy Tokar Miller, ink/paint images]. Tucson:
CHAX Press, 2007

S E C O N D LANGUAGE [collage: text by Kathleen Fraser; images by
JoAnn Ugolini]. Berkeley, CA: Cloud Marauder Press, 2009

ii ss [with Hermine Ford, mixed drawing and watercolor]. New York: Granary Books, 2011

ESSAY COLLECTIONS

Feminist Poetics: A Consideration of the Female Construction of Language. Unpublished manuscript, 1984
Translating the Unspeakable: Poetry and the Innovative Necessity. Tuscaloosa: University of Alabama Press, 2000

FOR CHILDREN

Stilts, Somersaults & Headstands [poems based on & illustrated with Pieter Brueghel's "Children Playing Games"]. New York: Atheneum, 1968

TRANSLATIONS

Lampi e Acqua [by Maria Obino; trans into English by Kathleen Fraser]. *AVEC*, 1993
"Introduction to Six Italian Poets" [trans by Fraser]. *Thirteenth Moon*, 1993

VIDEO

Women Working in Literature. San Francisco: SFSU Poetry Center, 1991

ARCHIVES

Archive for New Poetry, Special Collections and Archives of the Library at University of California, San Diego

NIGHTBOAT BOOKS

Nightboat Books, a nonprofit organization, seeks to develop audiences for writers whose work resists convention and transcends boundaries. We publish books rich with poignancy, intelligence, and risk. Please visit our website, www.nightboat.org, to learn about our titles and how you can support our future publications.

This book was made possible by a grant from the Topanga Fund, which is dedicated to promoting the arts and literature of California.

The following individuals have supported the publication of this book. We thank them for their generosity and commitment to the mission of Nightboat Books:

Elizabeth Motika
Benjamin Taylor

The editors of this volume are deeply grateful to Margaret Tedesco for helping to realize this book.

In addition, this book has been made possible, in part, by grants from the National Endowment for the Arts and the New York State Council on the Arts Literature Program.